O9-BTZ-521

SAY GOODBYE
TO POWERLESS
CHRISTIANITY

SAY GOODBYE TO POWERLESS CHRISTIANITY

Walking in Supernatural Surrender and Significance

CHÉ AHN

© Copyright 2009 – Ché Ahn

All rights reserved. This book is protected by the copyright laws of the United States of America. This book may not be copied or reprinted for commercial gain or profit. The use of short quotations or occasional page copying for personal or group study is permitted and encouraged. Permission will be granted upon request. Unless otherwise identified, Scripture quotations are from the New King James Version. Copyright © 1982 by Thomas Nelson, Inc. Used by permission. All rights reserved. Scripture quotations marked NIV are taken from the NEW INTERNATIONAL VERSION®, Copyright © 1973, 1978, 1984 International Bible Society. Used by permission of Zondervan. All rights reserved. Scripture quotations marked KJV are taken from the King James Version. Scripture quotations marked NASB are taken from the NEW AMERICAN STANDARD BIBLE®, Copyright © 1960, 1962, 1963, 1968, 1971, 1972, 1973, 1975, 1977, 1995 by the Lockman Foundation. Used by permission. Scripture quotations marked NLT are taken from the Holy Bible, New Living Translation, copyright 1996, 2004. Used by permission of Tyndale House Publishers, Wheaton, Illinois 60189. All rights reserved. Please note that Destiny Image's publishing style capitalizes certain pronouns in Scripture that refer to the Father, Son, and Holy Spirit, and may differ from some publishers' styles. Take note that the name satan and related names are not capitalized. We choose not to acknowledge him, even to the point of violating grammatical rules.

Dedication

To my loving wife Sue, and my wonderful children: Gabriel, Mary, Grace and Steve Baik, Joy and Kuoching Ngu.

Acknowledgments

The Lord Jesus, the One in whom I have placed my hope, deserves my greatest thanks in the writing of this book. He has not only taught me and shown me its truths, but His love has allowed the dreams described in these pages to come to pass. Thank you, Lord!

Words are so inadequate to express my deepest gratitude to Bessie Watson Rhoades who has been my personal editor for over ten years. Editing this book was a significant undertaking; Bessie had to fight through some personal health issues, yet she persevered to complete the project.

I am also grateful to Don Milam for believing in me and in this book. This is my first book with Destiny Image Publishers; I know it is the beginning of a wonderful relationship with this cutting-edge publisher.

Of course, I want to thank my family members, to whom this book is dedicated. Thank you for your sacrifice as Dad took time to write this book during our summer and winter vacations. I know that writing this book during these vacation times was not the best example to set; but there was no other time to do so. I ask forgiveness in the event my example causes anyone to stumble.

Finally, I want to thank the staff and the members of Harvest Rock Church, the best church in the world (I am slightly biased). Thank you for the rich revival history that makes this book possible. If it were not for you, there would have been nothing for me to write about.

Endorsements

We have known Ché and Sue Ahn for 15 years. They have always sought to be right in the middle of the fire and revival, and *that is where they want to take you.* We know of no better people to catch the impartation for signs, wonders, and the power of the Holy Spirit than Ché and Sue Ahn. We love them!

Ché's book makes it clear that it is the right of every believer to be filled with significance and power. Then he shows you how to be that world-changer. You'll truly miss out if you miss this! Read it for sure!

Wesley and Stacey Campbell
RevivalNOW! Ministry

Ché Ahn has been powerfully touched by one of the greatest outpourings of the Spirit in Church history. What encourages me most is that this move of God continues today, and this amazing story is still unfolding. By reading the profound truths of *Say Goodbye to Powerless Christianity,* we create the atmosphere for God to duplicate these ongoing miracle testimonies over and over again—through us! Read it without restraint! Read it ready to be changed!

Bill Johnson
Senior Pastor, Bethel Church
Redding, California
Author, *When Heaven Invades Earth* and *Face to Face with God*

I love Ché Ahn's latest book, not only because of its powerful content, but because of the lifestyle and character of the author himself. Not only is he a gifted communicator, Pastor Ahn is a genuine apostle of the Lord Jesus Christ today. My wife and I have been personal friends with Ché and his wife, Sue, for more than two decades and can testify to the integrity of this powerful couple. We recommend this book to anyone responding to God's call to make impact in the Body of Christ.

Georgian Banov
President, GlobalCelebration.com

Some people write, and some people take action; and occasionally we find a leader who has the ability to do both. Ché not only models greatness—he imparts the ability to do exploits. This book highlights important ideas and carries his DNA. It will change your opinion of yourself and your destiny. Get several copies and pass them on.

Lance Wallnau
President, Lance Learning Group

The spiritual candle of my life was lit early on while reading the histories of revival and biographies of great men. I know that the reading of God's story through the extraordinary life of my great friend, mentor, and confessor, Ché Ahn, will cause candles of prayer revival to be lit around the world. Out of failures and weakness the fires of earth-shaking prayer, signs and wonders, and apostolic expansion will erupt in your heart through this very real and humble man. This is *his* story, and it is my joy that some of it is our story together. Glory to God!

Lou Engle
President, TheCall

Transparent and *radical* are two words that describe this hard-hitting book by Ché Ahn.

With a prophetic glint, he chronicles the Holy Spirit's ruthless call upon his life to raise up an apostolic stream of revival to touch the ends of the earth, and he reveals secrets for every serious believer to walk likewise in power and significance. As you read, may your appetite be whetted with a holy desire for more of the Lord!

Jim Goll
Founder, Ministry to the Nations
Antioch, Tennessee
Author, *The Lost Art of Intercession* and
Encounters With a Supernatural God

In a day when we need powerful, supernatural Christians on the scene who understand their call, God has allowed Ché to write a book to train us. Ché Ahn not only has a heart for personal revival, but for territorial transformation as well. Recently, God caught me up in a vision and showed me fires moving in darkened places— first in the United States, then in other nations of the world. He called this the "Triumphant Reserve." Those are the ones who will be coming forth in days ahead, filled with fire and knowing God's glory. All of the Triumphant Reserve need to read this!

Chuck D. Pierce
President, Global Spheres, Inc.
President, Glory of Zion International
Harvest Watchman, Global Harvest Ministries

Say Goodbye to Powerless Christianity makes an incredible impact. Ché Ahn has opened his heart to us, and that enables us to change as well. I believe this book will bring personal and corporate revival to anyone applying its wisdom. I highly recommend it.

Cindy Jacobs
Co-founder, Generals of Intercession
Colorado Springs, Colorado

Ché Ahn followed us into the waters of revival, and he's still moving in the deep with his love of God. I've seen this man go from a "good" pastor to a world-changer full of the anointing and power of God, taking literally thousands with him. You can be one. Start reading today!

John Arnott
Toronto Airport Christian Fellowship
President, Partners in Harvest
Toronto, Canada

Ché Ahn's book, *Say Goodbye to Powerless Christianity*, is a powerful tool for all of us who want to stay in God's presence and walk in the fullness God intends. It is full of inspiring stories and powerful teaching. Thank God for a man who walks in beautiful authority and integrity. We stand together with him to cheer him on as he leads us forward into revival and reformation. If you, too, long for the restoration of the prophetic and apostolic Church which the Lord designed, read this book!

Heidi Baker, PhD
President and Founder, Iris Ministries

Table of Contents

Foreword

Are you seeing the big picture?

What I am referring to are the extraordinary ways that God's presence and power have been increasing among His people in recent times. It is important to see the big picture because we are living in a season of outpouring that is notably different from the seasons to which we have become accustomed in the past. In previous times, God's power came with a burst of light and a superstar revivalist—and all of it was followed by an afterglow. I think of many examples, including the Welsh Revival with Evan Roberts, the Fulton Street Prayer Meeting with Jeremiah Lanphier, and the Great Awakening with Jonathan Edwards.

What God is doing now seems to be different. Rather than a burst of light, we are experiencing a spreading fire. In biblical terms, we are seeing a river coming out of God's presence in the Temple and growing deeper and deeper as time goes on.

Yes, we have our events such as Calvary Chapel and the Jesus Movement, Vineyard, Toronto, Brownsville, Lakeland, and others. But when you see the big picture, you see all these as streams flowing into today's river of God.

I mention this because I want to point out that Ché Ahn, the author of the book you hold in your hand, may be unsurpassed as one who sees the big picture of revival and renewal in our generation.

What qualifies him to do this? Not only has he studied revivals and analyzed them, he has also been a personal and committed participant. He was saved in the Jesus movement, and he has ministered in all the high-profile revival events since. He, along with Lou Engle, founded TheCall, which has powerfully challenged youth to radical Christianity.

Back in the early 1980s, a young Korean-American pastor from Maryland showed up in my office when I was teaching in Fuller Seminary in Pasadena, California. As he cast his vision, he said he believed that God had assigned him to plant a charismatic church in Pasadena that would grow to 5,000. As he was saying this, I immediately liked this man named Ché Ahn, and I have liked him ever since. I was a professor of church growth; here was a person after my own heart.

I knew a bit about what he was undertaking. Pasadena had been a graveyard for charismatic pastors. None of the charismatic churches planted there had grown to any significance. But Ché changed history. Yes, it was very hard going at first. But he, along with Lou Engle as prayer pastor, hung in there. Things shifted when he started Harvest Rock Church in 1994, and now they own Ambassador Auditorium, a renowned performing arts center which some call the Carnegie Hall of the West. They have not quite reached 5,000 members; however, the apostolic network Ché has spawned, Harvest International Ministries, is now aligned with 5,000 churches in 35 nations! I'm proud of my student!

In *Say Goodbye to Powerless Christianity,* you will get to know Ché Ahn very well. Through his eyes you will begin to see the big picture of the fire of God. You will learn how to get yourself out of God's way and experience His power in salvation and renewal and miraculous healings and effective prayer and freedom through deliverance and prosperity in all that you do.

You will find out how you can be a history-changer!

C. Peter Wagner
Chancellor, Wagner Leadership Institute

Introduction

We all know that hindsight is 20/20. If ever—at the point in life when I felt like a failure—I could have imagined the life God still had in store for me, I would have boldly told others to "go for it" too.

Now I can say with confidence, "Pursue your dreams and follow the desires God has put in your heart. Step into the unknown to find even more!"

I was pretty happy being pastor of a steadily growing church. I was delighted to spend time with God, study the Word, lead others to salvation, train and disciple the flock. I was overjoyed at the privilege of going overseas with others from time to time to share the love and power of a sovereign God.

Those aspirations seemed pretty good to me. They were noble considering where I'd come from. I could never have dreamed that God would take me from being a 17-year-old rebellious druggie and son of a Korean Baptist pastor to where He has brought me today. If anyone else had envisioned such an outcome, I probably would have thought he was nuts!

There isn't a day that goes by that I am not in awe of what God has done in my life and how He continues to use me. As of this writing and by God's grace, I oversee Harvest International Ministry—which is comprised of more than 5,000 apostolic ministries in 35 countries. I am privileged to serve as Senior Pastor of Harvest Rock Church in Pasadena, California. We miraculously own the Ambassador Auditorium as our church—a building known as Pasadena's "Crown Jewel." It is one of the most beautiful and coveted arts centers in the United States; and God allowed us to steward it through a series of miracles. We give Jesus all the praise and glory for what He has done. We are amazed that we have television broadcasts and Internet webcasts that span the globe in more than 215 nations.

I have also been privileged to serve from 2000 to 2004 as President of TheCall, a solemn prayer movement that was founded by my good friend Lou Engle. TheCall hosted more than 400,000 young people and three generations on the Mall in Washington, D.C., in just one event and countless thousands more across the nation in recent years. TheCall is helping to bring change to the morals of our nation and government and is birthing a consecrated generation of youth radically sold out to God and His purposes for this generation. This same "call" has now gone to many nations around the world.

By God's grace, this is the ninth book I've written. I've traveled to 55 nations; and through those who have joined with us in this ministry, we have seen:

- *Christians placed in influential positions in foreign governments,*

- *Transformation in Hollywood,*

- *Orphanages built in desperate villages in the poorest of third-world nations,*

- *Street-gang youths of Los Angeles transformed into Holy Spirit-inspired, patent-selling inventors,*

- *A noodle factory established (operated by our ministry) to secretly feed starving North Koreans, and*

• *Severed body parts regrown through miraculous prayer.*

Many more stories like these are found in the pages of this book.

God has also been merciful to heal my own marriage. I have been blessed with a wonderful family. I love my wife. All of my children serve the Lord as the awesome adults they have become.

Not only do I have a fantastic family; I am also favored with friends whom I consider to be the Solomons of today.

Yet my most valued asset is my personal relationship with Jesus Christ and the consummate joy of His incredible presence.

In the final analysis, intimacy with God is the path to destiny fulfillment. The finest motivational speakers and the most successful personal trainers in the world can help you to become what you want to be. But I'd like to recommend a more exciting journey: follow the Holy Spirit so intimately that you hear His every breath and obey His every leading. Do this and the story you tell will be a story without end.

I had to learn this truth the hard way because, like many of us, I was convinced that self-effort was all that was needed. Save yourself the trouble and learn from my mistakes. All you need to do is *surrender to His lead,* just as Jesus did to His Father's. With your obedience, He will lead you where you thought you could never go.

My hope is that you will share your testimony with others as I am doing in this book so that they, too, will be encouraged to step into the incredible life and destiny to which they are called.

I pray that the accounts and transformations found in this book will enhance and prosper your life.

CHAPTER 1

Revived

Nineteen ninety-three was the worst year of my life. I know that sounds drastic, but that is exactly how I felt at the time—and it is the way I still feel today. After nine years of struggling as a pastor in Southern California, I had finally called it quits. I never thought things would turn out that way.

My Vivid Dream

Initially I had a lot of faith and vision for a great church. After all, God had literally given me a vision of coming to Los Angeles. It was more of a dream than a vision, but no dream had ever been so real to me. It seemed to be a summons from the very throne room of God.

My dream started in a fairly inauspicious way. At four o'clock in the morning of the second day of September 1982 (exactly three years from the date of my ordination), an African-American appeared to me in a dream and spoke these words: "The Lord wants you to come to Los Angeles, for there will be a great harvest."

I awakened, experiencing waves of the Lord's presence coursing through my body. The captivating words and melody of a song we sang at church played again and again in my mind: "the time of revival is here."

Immediately, I got down on my knees and began to pray. Finally, I could wait no more. Around 5:30 A.M., I awakened my wife Sue, and excitedly shared the dream with her.

Immediately, she bore witness to all I had seen. We were instantly united in our obedience to God's leading and began to spontaneously pray and rejoice in this new revelation.

Things were set into motion in our hearts beginning that day. Our plans seemed further ordained through more confirmations that followed. Just as Gideon asked the Lord for a clear sign that He was with him, so Sue and I threw out a fleece to the Lord.

We prayed that my best friend and pastor at the time, Larry Tomczak, would take the initiative to ask me if I wanted to plant a church, as I was also a member of his pastoral team. That would serve as my cue to share all that God had put into my heart about going to Los Angeles. It would be a pretty big move from Maryland!

Confirmation From Pastors

Six months after my dream, Larry asked me if I wanted to go out for lunch. I knew in my heart that this was the day Larry would ask me if I wanted to plant a church. I can't really tell you how I knew; I just knew. In the same way I was confident that my dream had been of the Lord, I knew He would confirm the dream that day.

Soon Larry and I were seated at lunch and I heard him say, "Ché, I'm sensing that we are too top-heavy with pastors in our church. I feel that we should send you out to plant a church. Do you have any desire to plant a church? If so, where?" he asked.

I could barely contain myself. "I thought you would never ask!" I exclaimed. I told him everything...the dream, the fleece, the call to Los Angeles.

"Los Angeles?" he queried incredulously. "I was thinking a little bit closer to home, like northern Virginia or someplace else close by," he added.

"Larry, I really believe this is of God," I affirmed. He seemed open to the idea and suggested I share it with our fellow pastors at our next meeting together. It would be the perfect time to find out what they thought.

As I shared, each of the pastors was similarly open to what I felt God was leading me to do. As a safeguard, they encouraged me to take some additional time to seek God and pray for further confirmation.

Confirmation From Television

To be sure about what we were hearing, my wife and I decided to get away and spend three days together in prayer and fasting. We borrowed my uncle's condominium in Ocean City, Maryland, a popular beach resort a few hours away on the Atlantic Ocean.

As we entered the condo, we set down our bags, knelt on the floor, and asked God to give us the confirmation we needed regarding a move to Los Angeles.

At that moment, in a passing flash, I had an impression that we were to turn on the television and that *The 700 Club* would be airing.

I said to Sue almost jokingly, "Honey, let's turn on the television and see if Pat Robertson is on. Maybe he'll have a word of knowledge for us." It wasn't typical of me to say something like that. In the natural scheme of things, it made even less sense. What were the odds that Pat Robertson's show aired in Ocean City, much less at that precise time of day? We didn't have a program schedule, and I wasn't sure the condo even had a working television set, as we happened to be visiting during the off-season.

The condo did have a television set, however, and it did work. Sure enough, as I began to flip the channels, *The 700 Club* was airing! I saw Ben Kinchlow and Pat Robertson praying over a stack of letters. Then they started to give words of knowledge, or specific impressions they were supernaturally sensing that God was saying (see 1 Cor. 12:8). Most of these words concerned various physical conditions the Lord was healing. Then Pat paused and gave this word of knowledge: "There is a pastor who is asking God for a confirmation about planting a church. The Lord says that this is of Him. And if you go out in unity and in harmony, the Lord will give you great success."

I couldn't believe what I was hearing. I shouted to Sue, "This is the confirmation we're looking for!" We were so ecstatic that we began to give praise to God and dance around the condo. Incredible! Then I had another idea. Perhaps the same edition of *The 700 Club* would air again later in the day on that same channel, as I knew it did at home. If so, I could tape-record that word of knowledge and play it later for my fellow pastors!

We kept the channel on all that afternoon and evening. Sure enough, the program played again. With portable tape recorder in hand, we were ready and the recording turned out perfectly. Grateful and confident that God had indeed answered our prayers for confirmation, we were able to celebrate and enjoy a wonderful mini-vacation, instead of fasting for three days.

The following Tuesday when I met with the other pastors, I shared exactly what had happened and played the tape for them. As one brother said, "I sensed the presence of the Holy Spirit during the playing of the recording. The idea of Ché and Sue going to Los Angeles is of the Lord." Having received the pastors' confirmation and blessing, we knew it would be only a matter of time before we would be sent to Los Angeles.

Sent to Pasadena

Los Angeles is huge. I am told that the total area of Los Angeles and Orange Counties would be equivalent to the number of square miles in

New Jersey and Delaware combined. So the question was, where in L.A. would God want us to begin? We had the comparable area of two states to choose from!

At that time, my friend Lou Engle gave me a book by Frank Bartleman entitled *Azusa Street*. It was Bartleman's account of the famous Azusa Street Revival that had taken place in the Los Angeles area around 1906 and spawned the Pentecostal movement.

Within a few pages, I was reading Bartleman's prayer, "Pasadena for God."[1] He wanted to bring the revival to Pasadena. As I read, the word *Pasadena* leapt off the page. I knew instantly that we were to go to Pasadena, but I didn't even know where Pasadena was!

I went to the library and began to research the L.A. area. I discovered that Pasadena was really the first suburb of Los Angeles. The nation's first freeway was built there, connecting the city to downtown Los Angeles. I also learned that Pasadena was the birthplace of many ministries, including Fuller Seminary, World Vision, Focus on the Family, and others. It seemed that God had long had His hand on this city, and I was thrilled that Pasadena was where the Lord was calling us.

Following a time of careful preparation and transition, my family and three other couples and a few singles were sent from Maryland to plant the new church in Pasadena.

At 28 years of age, I was ready to single-handedly bring another Azusa Street Revival to Los Angeles—or so I thought. Instead the trials began, and God started to break me.

Many times I found myself lying prostrate on the floor and crying. Instead of asking for the God of Elijah, I cried out for the "God of revival."

In Second Kings 2:14 it says,

> *Then he took the mantle of Elijah that fell from him, and struck the water, and said, "Where is the Lord **God of Elijah**?" And when he also had struck the water, it was divided this way and that; and Elisha crossed over.* (Emphasis added.)

Here, when Elisha asked to see the "God of Elijah," he was asking for the same miraculous signs and wonders that Elijah had experienced. Like Elisha, I cried out for the miraculous, for the God who had demonstrated His power in past revivals.

During this time, Lou Engle, David Warnick, and I began doing everything we knew to do. They would later become my fellow pastors and the three of us worked together exploring every way we could think of to fulfill the vision. No doubt that was part of the problem!

We held early morning prayer meetings for years. For the most part, it was a real challenge for me to rise early. I am more of a nightowl than an early-morning person. We had some seasons of outstanding prayer in which 40 or 50 people would pack the prayer room, basking in God's manifest presence. Yet, for the most part, we were dutifully "paying the price" and wondering whether our prayers were being heard.

On other fronts, we did everything possible to evangelize during that decade. We did open-air preaching at California State University, Los Angeles. We went witnessing door to door. We performed street theater. We went into the ghettos. We held special meetings at special venues with special speakers. Still we saw little fruit. Eventually, the church started to grow and God began to add some wonderful people to our group, but it was a far cry from revival.

Shaken by Circumstances

When a brother quipped, "The 1980s were from Hades," his words about summarized my decade. Given the scandals among television evangelists, it was not a fun time to be in the ministry. I feel it is important to share this time with you. Though it is long past, I believe it is an important puzzle piece in the journey God used to take me from despair to success. The Lord really knows what He is talking about when He says, *"The end of a thing is better than its beginning"* (Eccles. 7:8).

My own struggles at that time made things doubly difficult. When anyone asked me what I did for a living, I was tempted to tell them I was involved in sales or even insurance—anything but ministry! Then, as I was hoping for a difficult decade to end and a better decade to begin, things went from bad to worse. The bottom fell out completely!

The first cross-cultural church plant, sponsored by the larger ministry team of which I was a part, blew up in our faces. Without rehashing all the details, I will say that I was primarily responsible for what happened; it involved our overseas efforts. The end result was that missions were placed on indefinite hold in our church and in the organization as a whole.

Because our church had sent the missionaries and because we had built our church on a missions vision, many of our church members left. This change in direction left them disillusioned with both our local body and the larger church-planting ministry. More than 100 people left within a six-month period. I often wished I were among them, but the Lord would not release me.

Much good fruit did come from this ministry, but as my vision for the world seemed to evaporate, I experienced an indescribable devastation in my heart. Eventually a leadership change took place in the movement of which we were a part. The new leader made it clear to me that we were no longer going to plant churches in Asia or anywhere else outside of the United States and Mexico.

Ever since I was a young believer, I had had an intense burden for missions and for internationals; it fueled the majority of my pursuit of God and motivated all things to which I set my hand. The death of that vision caused me to begin to die, spiritually speaking.

Words fail to describe the passion and like-hearted commitment our team held so dear to see the Kingdom birthed around the world. Now, the emptiness I felt inside was equally intense. It was clear that the vision would never become a reality.

Somehow I made it to 1993. By January, however, Sue and I knew we were to resign as pastors and leave both the church and the larger organization. It was the hardest decision we had ever made in our lives. We had been with the founders of our movement for 19 years. It meant leaving the friends with whom we had built our closest relationships and with whom we had raised our children. This included our best friends, Larry and Doris Tomczak. To add to the awkwardness, my sister and my relatives were still involved with the mother church in Maryland.

A "Word" From the Lord

Sue and I knew God had spoken to us—and clearly. One of the ways He confirmed our move was through Cindy Jacobs, a leader and prophetess in the Body of Christ. The Lord woke her up and called her to intercede for us. Then God gave her a prophetic word (a specific directive inspired by the Holy Spirit) for us. (See Acts 13:1-3; 21:10-11; 1 Cor. 14:1.)

Cindy had never called us before. In fact, she had to call Dr. C. Peter Wagner, one of my professors from Fuller Seminary at the time to get our phone number. Cindy lived three states away and had no idea what was going on with us. No one knew, because we were waiting on the Lord for the timing and the proper way to share the changes. Cindy called and ministered a word to us about leaving our church and our movement; however, she said the move would not be until 1994. She also said that 1993 would be the hardest year of our lives.

Emotions flooded through me; they included the mixed feelings caused by receiving such a difficult word. It was somewhat comforting to know that my wife and I had heard a word from God about this most difficult decision and that it was confirmed by a well-known and respected prophetess. The disconcerting part was facing the hardship we would encounter. True to a part of the word Cindy shared, the "spaghetti soon hit the fan."

When I shared our decision with my fellow pastors and leaders of the movement, they were angry and disappointed. At stake were other issues of doctrine and philosophy of ministry upon which I would rather not expound. Ultimately, I no longer had faith to continue in a movement that had lost the original vision for world missions.

I was torn. I loved the people of the church, but how could I continue in a movement with which I no longer agreed? The Bible says in Amos 3:3, *"Do two walk together unless they have agreed to do so?"* (NIV).

It was the toughest decision Sue and I have ever made in our Christian lives. It felt like we were jumping out of a plane without a parachute. Still I knew the Lord would be our confidante and guide. Our desires were to obey His leading and to try to make the transition as painless for the church as possible.

A Difficult Transition Period

The leaders accepted my resignation as senior pastor, but asked me to stay for a one-year transition period. I agreed.

In all candor, I had no idea what was coming next. Although I knew God was asking me to resign and asking Sue and me to leave the church we had planted, nothing else was clear. All I wanted to do was sell our home and leave California. I wanted to be anywhere but Los Angeles.

Suddenly I found myself sinking into a deep depression. I had rarely been depressed, but it was obvious that I was really hurting. It felt as if the roof were caving in on me. My neck was wrenched in pain, and my body felt heavy and old under the stress. My family and I were suffering financially from the drastic salary cut. Without much success, I was trying to make up the income difference by doing itinerant work. It was a long and devastating six months.

We finally borrowed on the equity of our home to pay our bills. All the while, we were feeling rejected by our closest friends. Because it was our desire to move on, they also felt rejected by us. To top it off, I was mad at God for bringing us to California and not fulfilling the dream He had supernaturally given me.

I wanted to quit the ministry, move to a ranch, and train a watchdog to bite anyone who carried a Bible. Of course, I didn't really feel that strongly—but it was close! As I've said, nothing I could say at this point would do justice to all we experienced that year. I wouldn't wish the experience on anyone. That is why 1993 remains the worst year of my life.

As always with God, there was more to the struggle—and it would prove to be good in the long run. Although I didn't realize it during 1993, God was breaking me and preparing me for 1994—the year He would begin to fulfill the dream of promised revival.

Holy Laughter

In January 1994, Toronto, Canada, experienced an awakening that would be heard around the world. It continues even today! A major outpouring, or visitation of the Holy Spirit, had begun.[2] Many people do not realize that the same type of renewal hit the Anaheim Vineyard Christian Fellowship in California at the very same time.

The Anaheim awakening began on a Sunday night as the church was sending out their youth for a short-term missions trip. The Holy Spirit fell on the kids with unusually strong manifestations. Manifestations (various physical and emotional expressions that happen when a person encounters the raw supernatural power of God) often include laughter, crying, shaking, jerking, or the making of unusual sounds (see Jer. 23:9; Rom. 8:26; Rev. 1:17). Such expressions have been common in visitations of God throughout history.[3]

The following week, the Vineyard held its annual conference in California. That particular year the conference theme was healing. The featured guest speakers were Francis McNutt and Mahesh Chavda, two evangelists well known for their healing gifts.

The renewal from the week before spilled over into the conference in a powerful way. Lou Engle and I had registered for the conference and had no clue that a fresh revival was beginning in the Vineyard movement. We got tuned in quickly, however. On the first day of the conference, we saw with our own eyes the Holy Spirit falling on people and producing unusual manifestations of laughter, shaking, and other loud cries and noises.

Initially, I was cynical about what was occurring. I had read about Rodney Howard Brown and "holy laughter" in *Charisma* magazine; but I had never experienced this manifestation. I thought the people were laughing through mass suggestion and hysteria and not through a genuine move of the Holy Spirit.

One day during the conference, however, people seated in separate sections of the auditorium all laughed at one time as the Holy Spirit swept through the hall like a fresh wind. My friend Lou poked me with his elbow and yelled excitedly, "It's coming toward us! It's coming toward us!"

I remember saying, "Well, I'm not going to laugh." When the Holy Spirit hit our section, though, I felt myself becoming inebriated. I could not stop laughing. It lasted at least 20 minutes. Everything was funny...even though no one had said anything humorous!

A bald man was seated in front of me and, for whatever reason, his bald head looked funny to me. I leaned over and began to massage his head. He didn't care; he was laughing, too. It was a wonderfully refreshing experience that seemed to invigorate every part of my being. I didn't notice until later that my deep depression was gone!

How God moved on me surprised me as much as it must have surprised John Arnott in Toronto where it all began. As he puts it:

> We had been praying for God to move, and our assumption was that we would see more people saved and healed, along with the excitement that these would generate. It never occurred to us that God would throw a massive party where people would laugh, roll, cry, and become so empowered that emotional hurts from childhood were just lifted off of them. The phenomena may be strange, but the fruit this is producing is extremely good.[4]

The result of this experience bore immediate fruit in my life! I was revived! The word *revive* means "to restore to consciousness or life."[5] I had been depressed, depleted, and spiritually dead; now, I was alive. I was excited about ministry again. More importantly, I was once again in love with Jesus. I felt His presence, and I knew something incredible had happened in my life. Yet this was only the beginning of a life-changing week.

Empowered by the Spirit

The next day Mahesh Chavda spoke. He shared a dream he'd had the night before. He dreamt that a pastor brought two loaves of bread to the conference. Then he shared his interpretation of the dream: the pastor represented all the pastors at the conference. That was an interesting statement, since at least 500 of the 3,500 attendees were pastors!

The dream contained significant symbols. For example, the bread represented the healing anointing. Brother Chavda made references to the Syrophoenician woman who begged Jesus to come and heal her daughter. Jesus replied: *"It is not good to take the children's bread* [healing] *and throw it to the little dogs* [Gentiles]*"* (Matt. 15:26).

The woman responded saying, *"... Even the little dogs eat the crumbs which fall from their masters' table"* (Matt. 15:27). Noticing her faith, Jesus pronounced that her daughter was healed (see Mark 7:29-30).

Mahesh Chavda's point was that pastors were to take back to their home churches the healing anointing that was being imparted. As Mahesh shared his dream, I jumped out of my seat. When I left home that morning to go to the conference, my wife handed me two loaves of homemade raisin bread to take with me. I had never brought bread to a conference before and never have since!

Sue had simply been toying with a bread maker I had given her for Christmas and thought I might enjoy taking some loaves to eat and to share. When Mahesh began talking about a pastor who had brought bread, I wondered if the dream could be about me. I was trembling with anticipation and wonder.

As the session closed, Mahesh began to pray for people individually in a time of personal ministry. I made my way forward through the crowd to talk with him. As our eyes met, I said, "Mahesh, you don't know me, but I am a pastor and my wife gave me two loaves of bread to bring to this conference."

His eyes widened and he said, "You stay here!" He quickly went to the platform and grabbed a mike and said, "Ladies and gentlemen, may I have your attention!" A hush fell over the audience. "There is a pastor here who brought two loaves of bread, just like I explained in my dream. We are going to pray for him!" He walked up to me and placed his hands on my head.

All I can remember is that I went flying backward and landed on my back, shaking violently. That was the first time I had really been "slain in the Spirit"—or had the power of God cause me to fall to the floor (see John 18:1-6). Yes, I had gone down before when other leaders had prayed for me; but I have to admit I never felt anything. They were what I call "courtesy falls" (falling down even when you don't feel anything so as not to embarrass the minister or people who seem to expect it).

This time was different. I had never before experienced so much power through the laying on of hands. I used to be irritated with people in the Vineyard who would shake while praying—and now I was shaking uncontrollably! What is more amazing is that I have been shaking ever since that day! Whenever I worship or sense the presence of the Holy Spirit, my hands shake, sometimes more violently than other times. I don't fully understand these phenomena or manifestations, but it makes sense to me that if you touch raw electricity, your body reacts. If you touch the power of God, it should not come as a surprise that you react physically. When the supernatural meets the natural, a response will result!

Although it is not my purpose to give an apologetic for the manifestations that occur at revivals or renewals, I simply want to share what happened to me. I wasn't seeking to shake, but I did; and I have been shaking ever since. (For more information regarding these manifestations, I recommend the following books: *Catch the Fire* by Guy Chevreau, *The Father's Blessing* by John Arnott, *Let No One Deceive You* by Michael L. Brown, and *Welcoming a Visitation of the Holy Spirit* by Wesley Campbell.)

A Powerful Impartation Resulted

I also received a powerful impartation at the time Mahesh prayed for me (see 1 Tim. 4:14; 2 Tim. 1:6). I didn't realize it until I had a ministry opportunity the following week, when Lou Engle and I were asked to participate in a youth conference in Pasadena.

Throughout the youth conference, the Holy Spirit fell upon the young people just as we had seen at the healing conference the previous week. Kids shook and fell under the power of the Holy Spirit. I then realized that Lou and I had received something very transferable and wonderfully contagious. Yet what really shocked me took place in a seminar I held at the conference.

After I spoke, a young girl 13 years old or so came to me and said, "Could you please pray for my left eye? I am completely blind in that eye. I was at a carnival as a little girl and a metal object flew into my eye and severely damaged it. I have had three eye surgeries, and nothing has helped. I am completely blind in that eye."

As she was explaining her situation to me, I could feel what little faith I had begin to escape me. I honestly had no faith for her to be healed. I had prayed before for several people who had been blind and none of them had ever been healed. I expected this time would be no different.

As a pastor since 1979, I knew you prayed for people who asked for prayer no matter how impossible the situation might be. So I prayed. I remember asking her to put her hand over her eye, and I placed my hand over her hand. I don't even remember exactly what I prayed. It is not important anyway. What is important is that she had faith, and the Holy Spirit fell on her and healed her!

No words can describe what took place next. As soon as I removed my hand, she started to cry. "I can see your nose; I can see your face," she screamed. Incredulous, I exclaimed, "Really?"

"It's not totally clear, but my eye is open!" she cried. To say the least, I was totally amazed and shocked. I thought to myself, *What is going on here? Could this be the revival I have been praying for… the one God promised so many years ago?*

It wasn't long before I knew we were in the early stages of a historical move of God.

Endnotes

1. Frank Bartleman, *Azusa Street* (Shippensburg, PA: Destiny Image, 2006), 17.

2. Toronto Airport Christian Fellowship, *Spread the Fire,* January 1998.

3. Guy Chevreau, "Chapter 4," *Catch the Fire* (London, England: Marshall Pickering, 1994).

4. John Arnott, *The Father's Blessing* (Lake Mary, FL: Creation House, 1995), 59.

5. *Merriam-Webster Online Dictionary,* s.v. "revive," http://www.merriam-webster.com/dictionary/cry (accessed: February 20, 2009).

CHAPTER 2

Birthing an Apostolic Baby

T he transition was over. Free to pursue God's leadings, we began Harvest Rock Church in Pasadena with our fellow friends and ministers, Lou and Therese Engle. Lou had long held in his heart a dream of revival for Los Angeles, so he was the perfect partner for this new venture.

We began as a prayer meeting. If there's one thing I have learned, it is that you do everything by prayer and nothing without it. Every church must be founded on prayer, and that's just how Harvest Rock began. Our first answered prayer concerned the name of the gathering. My desire was to be a threshing floor of harvesting souls for the Lord, our Rock. *Harvest Rock* was a perfect fit.

We decided to invite extended family and friends who were not part of any church to come and pray. We weren't really sure whether anybody would come beside us. To our amazement, exactly 30 people came to our home the first Friday night in March, 1994. The following week, more than 65 people came and crammed into our living and dining rooms. I remember saying to myself, "Where did all these people come from? Who are these people anyway?" I hardly knew any of them!

Yet the Word became known because the Holy Spirit was there. We and our families had been moving in renewal, or this fresh outpouring of the Holy Spirit that had become known as the Toronto Blessing, since the end of January. We were simply inviting the Holy Spirit to attend our prayer meetings.

The meetings were very simple. We worshiped for at least an hour. I presented a brief teaching, and then we prayed for the new church. At the end of our prayer time, we prayed for the needs of the people. The Holy Spirit fell on many of the people attending. We could sense the power and the presence of the Lord. They were able to rest in the Holy Spirit and be empowered by His touch. You could see the peace on their faces and feel the gentle physical, emotional, and spiritual refreshing spreading throughout the room. Quite simply, that is why people came.

We missed taking a head count for our third prayer meeting in March, but the last Friday before my wife stopped counting we had 72 people packed like sardines inside our house. We knew we had to find another place to meet!

A pastor in Arcadia, a city next to Pasadena, offered a large building that had plenty of floor space in which to minister to our people. This was vital, because we found out early on that most people fell under the power of the Spirit when we prayed for them. To our dismay, the building was only available on Saturday nights, but we accepted it anyway.

At our first public meeting, more than 300 people came. We knew most of them were not looking for a new church; they were simply hungry for a touch of God and had come from other churches.

God presented Himself powerfully every week. Each Saturday night we prayed, and the Holy Spirit left the floor strewn with people gloriously caught up in the presence of the Lord.

We continued for a few months. Then I felt God requiring me to draw a line: we were to establish a church, not a prayer meeting. So I ministered a word about the formation of the church and asked those who were coming as members of another church to return to it unless they sensed God's leading to join Harvest Rock Church.

The following Saturday, only 150 people attended. I was not the least bit discouraged. I knew these faithful people were interested in becoming a part of Harvest Rock. We were not looking for a crowd; we were looking to build a church.

The growth of the church was not spectacular, but as 1994 came to a close, 250 people considered HRC their church. Taking into account the course of my ministry, I felt as though 1994 had turned out to be one of the best years of my life. I could hardly imagine things getting better than that. We were experiencing renewal, people were coming to Christ, and the church was growing.

However, 1994 would prove to be nothing compared to what was coming in 1995!

The Toronto Airport Vineyard Connection

The Christian community was abuzz about the new goings-on in Toronto, Canada.

People from all over the world were going to Toronto to experience the generous outpouring of the Holy Spirit at the Toronto Airport Vineyard Christian Fellowship. The presence of God was reported to be very thick; and many who had "come to the ends of their ropes" in ministry found a whole new start after receiving the impartation offered there.

In October 1994, Lou Engle and I finally made it to Canada for the "Catch the Fire" Conference. It was another life-changing experience. Many things happened at the conference; perhaps the most significant event was meeting John Arnott, the senior pastor of the Airport Vineyard.

Arnott had been catapulted into the international spotlight when renewal broke out in his church just months earlier, on January 20, 1994. I met him only briefly and informally. I happened to see him in the hall of the hotel where the conference was being held. In that instant of time, I asked him if there were any way he would come to Pasadena during 1995 and conduct renewal meetings. He informed me he had already received more than 300 invitations for the year and would probably not be able to come. However, he advised me to fax him an invitation anyway, saying, "You never know."

God knew, though! I went ahead and faxed a letter to John. Just weeks later, in December, I received a phone call from his secretary. John would be in San Francisco for the New Year's weekend. He would be willing to come to Pasadena for three days, but it would fall on a Monday through Wednesday. John wanted to know whether we were still interested in having him.

Without any hesitation I said, "Yes." Because of the suddenness of the visit, we didn't have time to advertise. Each week, however, I had been meeting with around 25 pastors for prayer, so I presented the idea of co-hosting the meetings with John Arnott in January. They all agreed.

We proceeded to rent one of the largest facilities in Pasadena: the Mott Auditorium. The building is named for the respected missionary statesman John R. Mott, who led the famous Student Volunteer Missions Movement in the United States in the early 1900s—a youth-mobilizing movement that quickly spread to the world and put missions on the map forever. The building is located on the campus of the U.S. Center for World Mission. The campus itself was founded by another missionary statesman, the late Dr. Ralph Winter.

Finally, the opening night of our meetings arrived! It was January 2, 1995; I will never forget what I saw as I entered the building accompanied by John Arnott.

More than 2,000 people had gathered for the meeting! It seemed like a reunion of Christians throughout the Pasadena area. I saw former church members and other people I had not seen for years. It seemed everyone I knew came, plus hundreds more I had never met. The power of God fell. The electric presence of the Holy Spirit permeated the meeting, along with signs, wonders, and healings (see 2 Chron. 5:13-14; Acts 2:43).

Renewal had truly come, not only to our church, but also to the greater Pasadena area. John Arnott helped us to firmly establish this move of the Holy Spirit in our city. (It has now spread around the world.) In retrospect, we would have to say that what we witnessed was revival. The fruit of that revival continues today.

At the same time that those early meetings took place, another series of divine events occurred. Three pastors joined their congregations with ours—notably, Pastors Karl and Debbie Malouff, who are our Executive Pastors to this day. Our shared heart and our common desire for revival in the city and nation drew us together in unity and the obvious blessing of God.

Another milestone was our merging with Rick and Pam Wright's Glendale Vineyard Church. Following that merger and after much prayer and confirmation from the leaders in the Vineyard, we became *Harvest Rock Vineyard* in March 1995. That wasn't the only major change to emerge from the meetings with John Arnott. John would suggest something else to us that would completely change our lives.

CHAPTER 3

The Power of a
Prophetic Church

I believe the key to any successful ministry is to be prophetically led by God Himself—that is, to do only what you see the Father doing (see John 5:19).

Many times we make our plans and ask God to bless them. The better way is to find out what His plans are and then align everything else with those plans. This is why those who abide in Jesus bear much fruit. As we wait on Him, He reveals His will. When we obey and follow His will, He promises us that we can be assured of bringing forth much fruit (see John 14 and 15).

This principle is a nonnegotiable tenet of my personal faith and that of Harvest Rock Church. Every significant blessing and breakthrough we have enjoyed is a result of obeying this principle, even when things don't make sense. Let me share some examples.

Renewal Meetings

When John Arnott conducted meetings for us at Mott in January 1995 and saw the number of people who attended, he immediately suggested we begin protracted meetings, just as they had been doing in Toronto since January 1994. I was not interested in Arnott's suggestion. Our church was less than a year old. In my natural mind, I reasoned that having meetings every night would burn out our people and eventually kill our young church.

The next month, we invited Wes Campbell to conduct meetings at Mott. He is another powerful brother who spreads revival across the United States. Again, the meetings were tremendously successful and much fruit was coming forth. Wes also encouraged us to consider protracted meetings. Sensing that God was saying something to us, and given the imminent merger with Rick Wright and the Vineyard, I opened up to the idea of hosting renewal meetings every weekend. I rationalized that after the merger we would have more available leaders and helpers to handle the additional sessions.

The objective was not to usher more people into our building, but to "move with the cloud" of God's presence and provide every opportunity available for Him to bless, refresh, and change His people. As I talked to my co-pastor Rick Wright about the idea of hosting meetings three times a week, he agreed, but also cautioned that more than three might not be healthy for our church. We decided to submit this suggestion to the rest of the pastors with whom we met weekly in prayer and to share with them our burden for renewal.

Surprisingly, we discovered that our conclusion about limiting the number of meetings was based on logic and natural thinking; God had other plans. Ironically, He used Rick to change our minds.

I will never forget what happened next. During our prayer meeting, the Holy Spirit began to prophesy through Rick. The Lord gave him the passage in Second Kings 13, where Elisha encouraged King Joash to strike the arrow on the ground. The king hit the ground three times. Elisha was furious that the king didn't strike more times. *"You should have struck five or six times..."* he shouted (2 Kings 13:19). As a result, the king won only three battles instead of winning a complete victory over his enemy.

Rick began to prophesy: "Just as when King Joash was told to strike the ground and should have pursued it five or six times, so we are not to have renewal meetings just three times a week—but we are to go five or six nights a week!"

The prophetic word was so powerful; everyone in the room bore witness that God had spoken. It also persuaded me to have faith to start the protracted meetings! John Arnott had agreed to come back to Pasadena in March, and we agreed that those meetings would launch the nightly revival meetings. So on March 24, 1995, we began. We met every night for 21 days. From then on, we met five nights a week for more than a year and a half. In the years since then, we have gone in and out of protracted meetings as the Holy Spirit leads. I know there is even more on the horizon.

Continuing to meet at Mott Auditorium, which we rented, was awkward for me. This had been the facility where the church I had founded and formerly pastored used to meet. Although they had moved from that particular building, they were located just across the campus from us on the U.S. Center for World Mission.

Yet because the protracted meetings involved several other churches and because Harvest Rock Church initially met in the neighboring city of Arcadia, it made the most sense to meet at the auditorium because of its large size and location. I would never have dreamed that the Lord would ask us to move our church into Mott. But that is exactly what happened.

Moving to Mott

"Ché, I know you don't sense this, but I really believe that God wants us to move our church into Mott." I must have heard that at least a half-dozen times from my friend and fellow pastor, Lou Engle. It wasn't because Lou lived across the street from Mott, which he did. Lou felt prophetically that Mott had been dedicated for revival by the Nazarenes some 60 years earlier, and he believed that God was going to visit it again. He sensed it was crucial for our church to be based at Mott in order to usher in and experience the fullness of the historic move of God we believed would happen.

Frankly, I wanted nothing to do with moving Harvest Rock—especially to a location just across the lawn from my former church. Emphatically, and almost angrily, I resisted the idea.

In addition, it made no sense to me to rent Mott for our church services. True, the protracted meetings were able to handle their share of the large building's rent, but having to pay more rent for the auditorium was a totally different proposition. After all, the Glendale Vineyard with whom we were merging was bringing with it a significant mortgage on the building it owned. Because we could meet there, it didn't make sense to rent Mott on Sundays.

God again would ask me to do that which boggles the rational mind. Meanwhile, I received a call from Jim Goll, a good friend and respected prophetic minister who lived in Kansas City, Missouri, at the time.

"Ché, I had a dream about you last night. I saw you holding a bottle of Mott's Applesauce...does this mean anything to you?" he mused.

"You wouldn't believe it if I told you," I replied. "Lou and I have been considering whether or not the Lord is leading us to move our church into a building called Mott Auditorium. As far as I am concerned, there is no way that we can afford it. Besides, it is too close to my former church. I just don't think it would be right to move there," I added with firm conviction. I thought I had done a pretty good job of at least convincing myself.

"Now I know what the dream means," Jim countered. "Ché, you are holding Mott in your hands. I believe God wants you to possess Mott Auditorium. The applesauce means you will bear fruit as you do. Furthermore, I am sensing that the Lord will provide for you, so you don't have to worry about your expenses—and He will also take care of your situation with your former church."

I must say that obeying God in moving into Mott Auditorium was one of the most difficult and humiliating decisions I have made since planting Harvest Rock Church. It was especially difficult because I had told the new pastor of my former church that I was not interested in moving into Mott. When God spoke, I knew I had to humble myself before that pastor and ask to be released from that word. I asked the Lord whether, in this situation, I should become one who swears to his own hurt (see Ps. 15:4) and not consider any move to Mott. However, through prophetic words and godly counsel, He directed me otherwise.

I had already made a commitment when we started the work that we would only do what we saw the Father do (see John 5:19), so I had to go forward with what He seemed to be saying now.

Just as holding protracted meetings made no sense initially, yet bore tremendous fruit, so I realize in looking back at the last few years that moving to Mott was also the right decision.

God would confirm His leading again a month after Jim Goll called.

An Angelic Visitation

On May 28, 1995, Mott experienced an extraordinary visitation. My daughter Joy, who was 12 at the time, and her best friend Christine, had just returned from the renewal meetings and were full of the Holy Spirit.

It was late when they came home, and I was just about asleep. Suddenly, I heard laughter and banging in the family room next to our bedroom. The girls were "camping out" on their sleeping bags in the family room, but were manifesting and shaking so much under the power of the Holy Spirit that they were thumping loudly on the floor.

Although this was wonderful and I was happy for them, they were making so much noise that I couldn't sleep. I had to get up early the next day and preach the Sunday message, so I needed a good night's rest. I went into the family room and politely asked them to be quiet. They apologized and said they would. I went back to bed. Fifteen minutes later, I heard more banging and laughing.

I have to be honest; by this time I was upset. I marched into the room and said sternly, "I'm glad you are having a wonderful time. But if you're going to manifest, go to your bedroom and manifest all you want. Just don't do it right next to my bedroom!" Once again they apologized, so I went back to sleep and didn't hear another peep. (Most parents would be thrilled to have such a "problem" with their children staying awake to spend time with God!)

I discovered the next morning that things became quiet because something far more wonderful happened. My wife, who had been helping me quiet the girls, realized the Holy Spirit was doing something unique with them. She listened while Christine began to prophesy, "Mott, Mott, we've got to go to Mott!" It was almost one o'clock in the morning. Not wanting to disturb me any further, and knowing the Lord was moving on these children, Sue drove the girls to the auditorium. The moment she unlocked the door to the building, she sensed the glory of God and saw a white mist and angels throughout the auditorium. The girls' eyes grew wide with awe. As they looked up, they began to describe seeing thousands of doves everywhere and hundreds of angels of every size and ethnic color!

Sue quickly went across the street and rapped on the Engles' door. Lou came over to Mott; he, too, sensed the strong presence of the Holy Spirit, but he saw nothing. Only the two little girls and Sue could see the angels and doves, along with flowers and other wonders. It was like a scene from the book of Acts, where angelic visitations were common.

Lou decided to separate the girls and test them to see if they were seeing the same thing. He would ask, "What are you seeing in that corner?" Each would say, "An angel." Then she would describe the very same angel without any collaboration from her friend. Sue also confirmed what they were seeing. Each saw and described flowers like no flowers that exist on earth. The flowers appeared as jewelry, but in vibrant colors they had never seen before. Christine and Joy saw thousands of doves. Several sat on each seat in the vast auditorium and many more were suspended from the ceiling.

They saw many other incredible things, but the most impressive to them were the angels. They described the angels as warring angels. They saw giant angels and infant angels as cherubs. This visitation lasted for almost six months. Other children also saw the angels at Mott. I asked my daughter to lay her hands on me, but I was still unable to see anything. God promised that He would pour out His Spirit on our sons and daughters, saying they would prophesy and see visions (see Joel 2:28). This is exactly what happened at Mott.

Our youth, however, were not the only ones guided by the Spirit's lead.

The Church Grows

We made it our aim to let the cornerstone of the prophetic be used to guide us in every decision we made at Harvest Rock Church. It is as Graham Cooke states in his book *Developing Your Prophetic Gifting:*

> Prophetic ministry is concerned with the church, and it is concerned with the direction we take, as well as who will lead and how we will get to our destination. Prophetic ministry brings God's perspective, releases vision and calling and undermines your enemy. It is concerned with the church fulfilling its call.[1]

The Lord did not disappoint us. I believe our obedience to follow His lead in choosing staff, locations, meetings, times, and more were all foundational in the Lord's choosing to trust us with more than we could imagine. That includes the birth and growth of Harvest International Ministry—our apostolic arm which now oversees more than 5,000 churches in 35 nations.

From basement prayer to merged congregations to worldwide networking? Only God could have seen that coming.

Leaving the Vineyard

Again I heard the Lord saying something that seemed to make no natural sense. As I mentioned, we had become The Harvest Rock Vineyard.

The Vineyard was precious to all of us, especially because John Arnott had come to help us start our protracted meetings and the renewal/revival that is still happening today in Los Angeles and in our related ministries worldwide. In fact, now historically termed a *revival,* this move which began in Canada is still actively flowing through thousands and thousands of ministries all over the globe. There are other revivals, too, that have been birthed in many other nations.

Yet soon after our name change, Jim Goll called again with another prophetic insight to share. As you have already seen, Jim consistently has significant and instructive words that proved foundational to us at Harvest Rock, but we would have to wait nine months to understand this one.

I was all ears. "Ché, as I was in my living room, I had an open vision pertaining to you. I heard a cork popping, and saw you with a rosé wine bottle. The words *nine months* were written on the front of the bottle. The bottle had been shaken and the cork popped out. The wine had changed inside the bottle. You were now holding another substance."

I dearly love the prophetic and I especially love Jim, but I didn't have a clue what he was talking about. What frustrated me more was that Jim had been given an interpretation of the word, but the Lord would not release him to share it with me. He said he would call in nine months to tell me the rest of the story.

In the interim, I forgot about the word. The next nine months presented myriad blessings and challenges that were consuming in their own right. The revival meetings were gaining momentum, but so was the criticism of people who did not like what was happening in Toronto and at Mott.[2] Many were calling this a counterfeit revival. In my opinion, the persecution and distractions adversely affected the national leaders of the Vineyard, which resulted in their request for the Toronto church to withdraw from its association with Vineyard.

Like many others, I was shocked at the request made of the Toronto church in October 1995. On December 8, Lou, Rick, and I met with the leaders of the Vineyard. We thought we would also be asked to drop our association with the movement. As we were driving to their headquarters in Anaheim, we discussed our options. I had just finished saying we needed to continue the renewal meetings, regardless of the outcome of our appointment. It was too obvious that God had initiated the work and that we must continue in it—even if it meant leaving the Vineyard. I concluded by saying, "At least we know that God has brought us together for this work."

No sooner had the words passed from my lips when a black Mercedes passed us bearing a license plate that read: "RICK CHE." Talk about a confirmation that our merger was God's doing!

I screamed, "Look at the license plate on that car!" Rick and Lou also started to scream and manifest as the Holy Spirit hit us. Although it may seem like a small incident to someone else, it served as a sign to us and gave us tremendous faith as we met with the leadership of the Vineyard. God seemed to be saying, "I initiated the renewal meetings. I brought the churches together. I am the head of Harvest Rock, and I am with you."

As it turned out, the leaders of the Vineyard did not ask us to leave. To quote a Vineyard leader, perhaps "a happy parting of the ways" might indeed be the best solution for everyone. We agreed amicably, for we were certain that all we had experienced as a result of our affiliation with John Arnott and Toronto was of the utmost continuing importance to us. Thus on December 7, Harvest Rock ceased to be a Vineyard church.

A week later, Jim Goll called. "Ché, do you remember the vision I had about you—the one with the rosé wine bottle with the words *nine months* written on the label…the bottle with the cork popped open?" he pressed.

"Yes," I replied haltingly, vaguely remembering the conversation those many months before.

"Here is the interpretation of the vision. But before I share it with you, I want to ask you how long you were with the Vineyard."

I remember having to count out the months on my fingers as I held the phone. "Nine months," I finally replied.

"Well, don't you get it?" Jim queried.

I still didn't know what he was talking about. Jim was happy to clue me in. "Well, the wine bottle represents your church. You were a 'Vineyard,' and after nine months, the cork popped open. I saw that the wine had changed and became a new substance. You were no longer a Vineyard. Get it? God told me through the vision that you would be part of the Vineyard for only nine months. I wanted to tell you the interpretation, but He wouldn't let me. It could have been interpreted as being divisive if I had told you beforehand that you would be leaving the movement within such a short time. That is why I could only share the vision and then wait nine months to give you the interpretation," he concluded.

I was absolutely stunned by this. Several things went through my mind. My first thought was that Jim is an incredibly prophetic brother who receives accurate specifics from the Lord. I was very grateful for the tremendous comfort and encouragement his words had given me.

God in His sovereignty had indeed called us to become a Vineyard church—and then had sovereignly led us out. We followed Him both times, and both times it was His will.

There is no substitute for the peace you have in knowing God is with you in the difficult transitions that often accompany ministry. How anyone can lead without the grace and support found through solid prophetic revelation and confirmation is a mystery to me.

Thank God He chooses to use this vehicle of ministry. As Dr. Bill Hamon says, "The prophetic ministry is one of the nearest and dearest ministries to the heart of God."[3] God wisely chose the prophets and apostles to be the directional and structural foundation of the Church, with Christ Himself as the Chief Cornerstone (see Eph. 2:20).

To this day, I am thankful that God did lead us to be a Vineyard church, even though it was for such a short time. I love the Vineyard movement and its leadership. I have no doubt that our unique "spiritual DNA" was developed in part through many wonderful values we received from our association with the Vineyard movement.

I am also grateful that God led us on from the Vineyard because He had other plans and another movement. It would be a movement He would allow me the privilege of starting and leading—and one that would encompass what He had placed in my heart many long years ago.

It would be a vision for the nations.

Endnotes

1. Graham Cooke, *Developing Your Prophetic Gifting* (Kent, England: Sovereign World International, 1994), 194.

2. Michael L. Brown, *Let No One Deceive You* (Shippensburg, PA: Revival Press, 1997).

3. Bill Hamon, *Prophets and Personal Prophecy* (Shippensburg, PA: Destiny Image, 1987), 17.

CHAPTER 4

A Vision for the World

In April of 1995, Harvest Rock Church had joined the Vineyard, presumably for life. We had no intention of joining or starting another movement. Why reinvent the wheel? The Vineyard loved the renewal and was planting churches around the world. The late John Wimber had personally shared with me a desire to plant 500 churches in Asia alone, and he wanted me to play a major role. I was sold; so we became a Vineyard church. Who would have guessed that we would be out of the Vineyard after only nine months?

Life is not perfect; nor is it predictable. People change and so do movements. When the leaders asked John Arnott and the Toronto church to leave the movement in December of 1995, we thought it would be best for us to leave too. It seemed that neither John nor I still had the Vineyard "DNA." Now the big question became: *Where do we belong?*

I had always believed in accountability and spiritual covering. The natural decision was to go with John Arnott. John was planning to start his own apostolic network, which he eventually did, called Partners in Harvest. A number of Vineyard churches left when the Toronto church was ousted, and they immediately looked to John and Carol Arnott for leadership.

Many independent churches affected by the Toronto Revival also joined Partners in Harvest as soon as they heard about it. In addition, John had personally invited me to be part of the new movement. It made total sense to join Partners in Harvest. After all, we were both from former Vineyard churches that loved the revival.

In a sense, John had also been the spiritual father of our own revival meetings. He had been the first to help us organize the citywide gatherings in Pasadena. In addition, we deeply loved and respected John and Carol and had become good friends with them within a short time.

John planned an inaugural meeting with pastors who were interested in the Partners network. The meeting was set to coincide with the third anniversary marking the birth of the Toronto Revival. I bought my airline ticket and prepared to fly to Canada in January to join the celebration and officially join Partners in Harvest.

Again, I received a phone call that would change all my plans. But that's what the principle of doing only what you see the Father doing is all about!

Prophetic Word: A New Apostolic Network

Up to that point, I had received only one phone call from my dear friend and sister, prophetess Cindy Jacobs. She had shared the amazing and accurate prophetic word regarding my departure from the first ministry organization I had served for many years. Now, at the end of December 1995, she called again. Cindy had heard that we were no longer a Vineyard church. Once again, she delivered a strong prophetic directive that would change the destiny of our ministry.

"Ché, you are not to join another movement. The Lord has called you to be a *father* of your *own* movement. He has called you to be an Abraham, and out of your loins you will be a father to many. You will have churches in every continent says the Lord," she declared.

Her words exploded in my heart. Years earlier, Ralph Mahoney, the founder of World Map, had given me the same word. In fact, I had kept a written copy of it. I had often pondered his word in my heart, just as Mary of old did (see Luke 2:19). Yet because of my own insecurities, I did not see how it could ever come to fruition. Now I was hearing it again. Things had changed, and my plans to be a Vineyard church for life had fallen through. I knew that God had something else in store for me—but starting my own movement was the farthest thing from my mind!

Though I still had my doubts, something inside told me this was a word of the Lord. When I shared it with my wife and the pastoral staff, each bore witness to its accuracy. My fellow pastor Rick Wright, himself a prophet, said that we should not only obey the word, but should also share it with John Arnott. So, in late January, Rick and I flew to Toronto for the scheduled kickoff of Partners in Harvest. In addition to this celebration, a meeting was scheduled for other leaders from around the world; these were leaders who were interested both in networking the renewal to other parts of the globe and in providing international leadership for it.

It was an honor to be in these gatherings, but I was very apprehensive about meeting with John Arnott. I was not looking forward to sharing the news that we were no longer planning to become part of Partners in Harvest. I was hesitant because similar encounters with other people in my past had ended in rejection. Had I known how gracious John's response would be, I never would have given it a second thought.

When we did speak, I shared the word and what I believed God was speaking to me. John and Carol responded with a most godly release. We all shared disappointment that we would not be working intimately together, but both of them encouraged me to follow God's prophetic leading.

To this day we remain very close to the Arnotts. They have not only opened their pulpit to us in Toronto, but we often share the same platform all over the globe. They are some of the most loving and anointed people I have ever met. No wonder God continues to use them powerfully around the world.

To this day and beyond, the flavor of the Father's love that emanates from the revival in Toronto can be found from the most distant fields of Africa to the underground house churches in China. Countless national and international leaders remain transformed by the work of God through this move; and many hungry people travel to Canada even today for that impartation.

Harvest International Ministry

We needed a name for our apostolic network. Again, I don't know whether God inspired the name or it was breathed from my spirit, but *Harvest International Ministry* came to me loud and clear.

It seemed to be the perfect ministry name for two reasons: First, we were believing God for a great international harvest. Second, the first letters of each word spell out the acronym *H-I-M*. That aspect of the ministry name fit our vision because the ministry was to be all about Him—Jesus.

We did a legal search for the name, and to my surprise, no one was using the name in California. So we incorporated as a nonprofit mission agency. HIM was born. The vision I'd always held—of going to the nations and sharing the Gospel of the Kingdom—was now becoming a reality.

God was also placing in my heart ideas for how the vision would happen. The New Testament apostolic church model that impresses me today existed long ago, in the first century at Antioch. The Antioch church sent Paul and Barnabas as their first apostolic team to plant churches in unreached areas of the known world at that time (see Acts 13). The Antioch church consisted of a plurality of multiethnic and prophetic leaders committed to worship, prayer, and missions.

We had begun Harvest Rock Church on the same premise. We taught that the church existed for missions. Our vision was to send church planters throughout the world. We also believed it was providential for Harvest Rock to be located on the campus of the U.S. Center for World Mission. The Center's founders, the late missionaries Ralph

Winter and his wife Roberta, brought great clarity to the Body of Christ and much fruit from the Great Commission by targeting the remaining unreached people groups and keeping them as their focus.

This clearly defined our priority for HIM. The first apostolic team officially sent out by Harvest Rock Church and HIM were Jamie and Chiho Harris. They were sent to an unreached people group of 2.5 million people in Asia. For security and safety reasons, I am not at liberty to say anything more about the work.

Though unreached people are certainly a priority, God made it clear that He wanted us to plant churches in frequently-reached nations as well. We were simply to work wherever the Holy Spirit directed.

One thing God has made clear is for us to invite other churches to partner with us in fulfilling the task. We realized that as a local church we could only do so much. If we networked with hundreds of other like-minded churches, however, we would have enough resources to cause serious damage to satan's kingdom. We would accomplish this by planting churches around the world. We not only want to be a part of what God is doing today; we also want to be part of the way God is doing it.

Dr. C. Peter Wagner, my mentor and an internationally respected leader in church growth, views it this way:

> Church growth analysts are beginning to identify apostolic networks as a modern movement. World-changing leaders and movements are arising to establish progressive structures for families of churches and ministries.[1]

That is the very reason our October "Catch the Fire" conference at Mott Auditorium in 1996 became a watershed week for HIM.

We invited several independent churches to meet with us a day before the conference officially started. We shared the vision of HIM and invited any interested churches to be apostolically aligned with us. To my surprise, many did.

I never could have imagined just how HIM would grow. We went from sending the first couple to an unreached people group in Asia to having more than 5,000 affiliated churches and ministries in 35 nations!

Many of the affiliates included in this tally are counted as a single organization when they are, in fact, apostles in their own right overseeing hundreds of churches in their own networks. HIM has become an apostolic network made up of other apostolic networks. That is why we have grown so much since 1996. It is not that every church in the network looks directly to me for oversight as their apostle; but each church's apostle does.

We know we are only one of many apostolic networks God is raising up as wineskins for the great harvest. We're simply delighted to be a part! Yet the continued response of like-hearted and sincere world-changers continues to amaze me. I believe I am privileged to serve with the most incredible group of Spirit-led, humble, loving, fire-breathing world-transformers the earth has ever known!

Line space and security reasons prohibit me from naming our leaders and their networks here. Whether it's a network of 500 churches in India, a single church of 50 or of 8,000, a group of 40 churches in Tanzania, our U.S. apostles serving in South America, the Philippines, or anywhere else around the globe—these participants are shaping the kingdoms of this world for Christ (see Rev. 11:15).

We have moved well beyond our initial vision to simply plant churches. We now realize that if we confine our influence to the area within church walls, we are not doing all we can to bring Heaven to earth (see Matt. 6:10) and cause the reality of Jesus Christ to impact every area of society.

In fact, at this year's major HIM conference, we hosted a dear friend, Lance Wallnau. Lance is a respected authority and speaker (both in the Church and in the marketplace) on the subject of how to transform culture. We had our leaders from around the world attend the Pasadena conference; they learned not only about the need to reach beyond the walls of church to society, but also about the mandate and wisdom needed to do it.

God is God of all, and He is tired of humanistic, selfish man claiming the forefront in the "seven mountains of society"[2]: education, government, media, the economy, religion, arts and entertainment, and family. God's intent is for *His* people to be in the forefront of all societal realms.

This touches directly on the Great Commission in which God commanded us to *"make disciples of all nations"* (Matt. 28:19 NIV). This cannot be done on the strength of a mere passing exposure to the Gospel or by leading just a few souls to conversion. Making disciples of all nations occurs when God's values are brought into every one of these societal institutions.

That is why we are encouraging every one of our members, their churches, and families to take seriously the call that is on their lives. An excellent Christian news reporter is just as much a minister as a man in the pulpit. A godly actress who brings truth to the public is a transformer of society. A married couple who press past selfish inclinations in order to stand firm in the irrevocable bond of marriage also accomplish the establishment of God's Kingdom priorities on earth. A man with Solomon's wisdom in times of economic hardship equally reflects God's dominion.

This revelation is expanding the work of HIM day by day. We now have members who have successfully run for parliament in their respective nations; others are nearing the top of the ladder in their government roles; many have children and congregations actively engaged in pursuing their place in one or more of these "mountains" of society.

God said that His mountain would be the chief among mountains (see Isa. 2:2-3). He has left us to obey His assignment to that end. We are currently in the process of understanding the huge scope of what God has called us to do in the nations. While saving souls is great, *discipling nations* is better! We have set our faces like flint—and that's where we are headed.

The New Apostolic Reformation

C. Peter Wagner's latest book on apostolic ministry is *Apostles Today*. In it he argues convincingly that we are in the second apostolic age. He says we are seeing a new "apostolic reformation" taking place. He defines this reformation as a new implementation of church government as outlined in the Bible. (Wagner says this is not to be seen as a denominational move reflected in church titles, such as Pentecostals used in naming The Apostolic Deliverance Pentecostal Church.) This new apostolic reformation in the truest sense means that there are clear apostles leading networks; they are bringing reformation to society and the Church, much as the Protestant Reformation did.[3]

We know that God intends for there to be an end-time revival that will overshadow any in previous history. In His wisdom, He set forth the structure which could oversee and contain such a move and reformation.

Because I am called to the role of the apostolic, I want to look at this reformation in the context of where the Church is going. The Bible says that the Church is *"built on the foundation of the apostles and prophets, with Christ Jesus Himself as the chief cornerstone"* (Eph 2:20 NIV). Wagner comments:

> ...In the nuts and bolts of the growth and development of the Church after He ascended and left the earth, Jesus apparently prefers to be thought of not as the *foundation* but as the *cornerstone*. The foundation of the Church through the ages is to be made up of apostles and prophets. The cornerstone is essential because it is the primary building block, the identifying, central stone that holds the foundation together and guides the laying of all subsequent blocks that go into constructing the building. If a church has Jesus *without* apostles and prophets, it has no foundation from which to initiate solid building. The two go hand in hand; there cannot be one without the other.[4]

This is a critical hour for the apostles and prophets to take their places. Another way of seeing the two offices working synergistically is Dr. Bill Hamon's view. I have often heard him cite the apostles as the "architects" and the prophets as the "building inspectors." It makes sense for both to be necessary for the building of God to be well established and eternal.

Dr. Wagner, commenting in David Cannistraci's book *Apostles and the Emerging Apostolic Movement,* believes "we can begin to approach the spiritual vitality and power of the first-century church only if we recognize, accept, receive and minister in all the spiritual gifts, including the gift of apostle."[5]

Wagner believes one way to recognize a modern-day apostle is to find a person who is looked to by many churches for leadership. Usually these churches are ones the person has helped plant either directly or indirectly. Or they may have the ability to pull apostles from different networks together to convene for a purpose; an example is what James did in Acts 15 at the Jerusalem Council.

C. Peter Wagner calls these "horizontal apostles,"[6] or apostles that convene other apostles together. Peter Wagner himself is a "horizontal apostle." Harvest International Ministry is what Wagner calls a "vertical apostolic network."[7] As I said earlier, we are a network of networks. At this writing, we have commissioned 23 apostles to oversee their respective networks in different parts of the world.

To be frank, I have not tried to build my own network. I have simply tried to advance God's Kingdom by releasing or giving away networks to other apostles. As a result, God has tremendously blessed these ministries. Truly, if we *"seek first His Kingdom and His righteousness..."* (Matt. 6:33), He will take care of the growth and the sphere of one's apostolic ministry.

I am just honored and privileged to be part of what God is doing and saying to the Church today!

Endnotes

1. David Cannistraci, *Apostles and the Emerging Apostolic Movement* (Ventura, CA: Renew Books, 1996), 188.

2. For more on Lance Wallnau's teaching on the "seven mountains," visit his website at http://lancelearning.com.

3. C. Peter Wagner, *Apostles Today* (Ventura, CA: Regal Books, 2007), 6-9.

4. *Ibid.,* 11.

5. Cannistraci, 12.

6. Wagner, 79.

7. *Ibid.,* 77.

CHAPTER 5

Raising the Bar
for Healing

"**P**astor, we think our friend is demon-possessed!" (See Luke 8:27.) "Would you please come and minister to her?"

My heart sank. It was only our second citywide revival meeting in Pasadena. More than 1,000 people had come that particular night. People were being ministered to wonderfully and joyfully on the gymnasium floor of Mott Auditorium. The last thing I wanted to do was to shift gears and pray for someone's deliverance. Yet I quickly followed the small band of Korean students who had come to me for help.

A Korean Student's Miracle

They led me to another Korean student who was approximately 20 years old. She was lying on the floor clearly manifesting something, but I discerned that the manifestation was not demonic. Instead, it was a powerful touch of the Holy Spirit. She was shaking and speaking in tongues.

I immediately reassured her friends that this was not the work of the devil, but the sovereign hand of God. I encouraged them to remain with her and pray for her as she continued to receive from the Lord.

Because this visitation was so new to everyone, there were many people early on who thought that some of the manifestations looked demonic. We soon learned from the fruit of changed lives and marvelous healings that these unusual displays were from the Holy Spirit (see Matt. 12:33).

This proved to be true in the case of the Korean student. I didn't know what had happened to this young girl until a few weeks later when her pastor told me about it. He had come to Mott with his whole congregation. He helped pray for this young congregant and witnessed all that happened.

He explained that this student had severe scoliosis and was, in fact, encouraged to have surgery. While she was on the floor at Mott, God gave her a new prayer language and healed her back!

The following week when the doctors took X-rays, they were dumbfounded. They could not believe that her back was straight. She asked the doctors to give her the X-ray films; she brought them to her pastor to show him the results of prayer that night at Mott. The pastor was so impressed that he not only shared this story with me; he also felt led by the Lord to sow into what God was doing in the ministry. He gave us a check for $4,000 to support the revival meetings at Mott! This is only one of many incredible miracles that have occurred.

A Miracle Healing of Multiple Sclerosis

Another is the story of Brenda Quintero, who shares her words firsthand. Brenda and her husband are pastors in our HIM apostolic network.

A few years ago, I felt like I was given a death sentence. I was diagnosed with multiple sclerosis (MS). It is a neurological disease that affects the central nervous system. The body begins to destroy itself, one nerve and muscle at a time.

There was really nothing that the doctors could do to stop the progress of this horrible torment, except advise me to avoid stressful situations. While that seemed impossible to anyone living in this day and age, I tried to more effectively manage my stress. As a real estate agent, I needed to show property to clients, but eventually I could not even do that because my right foot would drag. Soon, even walking up and down the steps at my office became difficult, so my desk had to be moved to the ground floor. All the while, satan repeatedly whispered things like, "You rebelled against God. You put other things first. After He died for you, you counted His death for nothing. You can't be healed. You don't deserve His kindness." The words weren't always the same, but the message was clear. I was a born-again Christian and believed with all my heart that God could heal me. But eventually I gave in and agreed with the accuser's lies, thinking that I was not worthy of God's mercy and healing hand.

After a couple of years of living under these lies, I realized that I did not have to be perfect to receive from God. God began a transformation in me as He showed me tangibly His love and His wonderful presence night after night through the renewal meetings and the Word coming forth every day. I prayed anew that He would take complete control of my life and admitted I had been rebellious. The Lord began a deep cleansing in me and gave me a double portion of His Holy Spirit. As I yielded and obeyed God more, His presence in my life increased and became more and more real as the months passed. It is like I became a "reborn" born-again believer!

Even though things were changing on the inside, nothing had changed for the better in my body. In fact, things seemed to get worse. I had just experienced a particularly bad day for me physically. I had to lean on my husband to make it into the renewal services at Mott Auditorium. As I was listening to the message, my right leg began to spasm uncontrollably.

I cried out before the Lord to remove this abomination from me. Later, a dear friend of mine told me, as I was crying out, that the Lord would heal me when it would give Him the most glory. I suddenly began to think of all the stages of MS: a walker, a wheelchair, then being bedridden.

I reasoned that the most dramatic healing would be after I became bedridden, so I prepared myself for this probability.

Two days later at Mott, a woman who was blind in one eye and had only partial sight in the other eye was healed. When I saw the power of the Lord at work and felt the incredible anointing of the Holy Spirit, I asked my husband to pray for me right that second. I fell to the floor under the power of the Spirit and lay resting there for a few minutes as others around me did as well.

Soon, I got up and went to take my place as part of the prayer team to minister to others who had come to receive at the meeting. I didn't notice anything different than I had felt at any previous times of prayer.

About 11 P.M., I had finished praying for others when the Lord spoke loudly into my spirit and said, "Take off your shoes and run." I reasoned with God saying that if He hadn't healed me, I would fall flat on my face. Again I heard … "Take off your shoes and run." I decided to go for it! I took off my shoes and went full speed ahead! It was absolutely incredible! I didn't fall! In fact, I ran around the auditorium twice before I came to my husband and said breathlessly, "Honey, I think I'm healed!" My husband asked me to run again— so I did! Then we began telling everyone what had just happened! It was a miracle— God had healed me!

I really can't describe the change. Two days earlier, I had taken a hard fall while just walking through my house. Now I was running! I was doing things I hadn't done in years—I skipped, I jumped, I ran, and I danced before the Lord—laughing all the while because the enemy was defeated! I'll never be the same—body, soul or spirit! God's mercy triumphed—and He healed me! Praise the Lord![1]

This was early in the revival. I can enthusiastically report that many years have passed since Brenda ran around our auditorium; she is doing well and the doctors still cannot find MS in her cat scans!

Brenda was not the only recorded healing of MS we have seen through Harvest Rock Church.

Glory to God! Others had to hold on in faith for their healings, too. Their miracles also came at Mott.

Another Remarkable Healing in Its Time

One such miracle was received by Louis. He came up to me in the prayer line on an Easter morning. At first I thought he had broken his wrist because he had his hand bandaged and his arm was in a sling. I asked him what had happened to him.

He told me that he'd had an accident over the weekend and his finger had been cut off from the second knuckle down. The digit had been completely severed and could not be reattached.

Regrettably, the mishap had occurred as his teenage daughter was helping him trim the hedges in the yard. She unintentionally cut off his finger while wielding the hedge clippers.

In the prayer line, Louis showed amazing faith and said, "Pastor, I believe God wants to grow my finger back, and I want you to stand with me in faith." I agreed with him, hoping for the best.

A couple of months later, I could see him after the service coming back through the prayer line. I have to be honest; I totally forgot what had happened because I guess I didn't believe the finger would grow back. I thought he might be coming back to ask for more prayer about it.

As he got closer, I could see a smile on his face. As he reached me, he held up his hand to show me his brand-new finger—with a new nail bed and all! I repented on the spot for my unbelief and celebrated the miracle with him. Even greater was the fact that his daughter, who had been fighting guilt since the accident, gave her life to the Lord when she witnessed God's restorative power!

Believing God for the Miraculous

I can honestly say that I witnessed more people healed in the first three-and-one-half years of the revival than the previous 21 years of walking with the Lord. Now, after 15 years since the start of the revival, I still believe it is only the beginning. I know God intends for *every one of us* to move in this kind of power to heal. After all, Jesus said these signs *"will follow those who believe"* (Mark 16:17). That means *all* those who believe!

In the past two decades, we have heard so much about the nameless, faceless generation—that God is using ordinary people, people who are nameless and faceless, not Christian celebrities. It is actually happening. Don't miss out on your opportunity to be part of what God is doing. It simply requires faith and trust and a *lack* of self-effort. It is God who does the healing. You are a conduit. Go for it!

Let the following word prophesied some years ago by Cindy Jacobs in her Generals of Intercession Newsletter encourage you:

> This is a crucial hour for My church when I desire to pour out My glory in a greater measure than has ever been seen. Satan is trembling and working diligently to get you to doubt Me because of the wave of glory and miracles I am getting ready to pour forth across the earth. Signs and wonders will come to the church, not just trickles, but in a flood: a flood of the miraculous. You will see the dead rise, the deaf hear, and the blind see. Once again the ambulances will bring the people to the church because I am the God of the impossible. Believe me. Declare war on unbelief and get ready to receive the flood of the miraculous that will sweep thousands of souls into the Kingdom.[2]

I couldn't agree more. It is time for the Church to declare war on unbelief and believe God for the miraculous. It is time to believe for the sake of those who suffer, but even more so for the sake of those who are lost. Miracles, signs, and wonders are one of God's most potent tools to reach the lost. *The greatest miracle of all is still that of a soul coming to Christ.* I believe that we are in the beginning stages of the greatest harvest of souls the Church has ever seen. This revival is about the Holy Spirit releasing the power to win the lost. I saw that beginning in the very early days of Harvest Rock Church.

The signs and focus on evangelism are mandates for every believer and an invitation for believers to take their rightful place as representatives of Christ in this world. That means *all of us* have His power within us to demonstrate the miraculous in many ways *every day*.

As Pastor and close friend Bill Johnson likes to say, "We need to come to the place that we are so used to living supernatural lives that it just becomes natural." That is starting to happen. We have hundreds of people in our church body who take God at His Word; their results speak for themselves—miracles! I would go to any one of them for healing prayer as quickly as I would ask another healing evangelist to pray for me.

Another wonderful testimony involves a member's home group. It's the last testimony I'll share here only because space does not allow for more.

Irene had struggled against Guillain-Barre Syndrome—a potentially deadly and painful muscle disorder; she also had CIDP, a related inflammatory disorder of the nervous system. These ailments had taken a severe toll on Irene's body and particularly on her heart, which was giving out.

After years of fighting for her healing, Irene's faith had also weakened. She was ready to give up. One day, the Lord quickened her to go to a home group meeting down the street from her home. It was led by some people from Harvest Rock Church.

In pain and agony, Irene slowly made her way to her neighbor's home. She said she'd never forget the prayer that was prayed. The anointing oil and sweet smell of the Spirit of God came all over her. Though she didn't feel any physical improvement at first (she struggled to get home that night), Irene was encouraged and had renewed faith that God would heal her.

The next morning as she got out of bed, Irene slowly lowered both legs to the floor. She noticed there was no pain! She started poking her legs—and still no pain. This had not been the case for years! She got up and started running. Then she started screaming and crying because she knew she had been healed! Her kids rushed in to see what was wrong. She screamed, "I'm healed!"

Then Irene *ran* to her neighbor's pool, jumped in, and began swimming! She was ecstatic because she was performing movements that had been impossible to her. Irene's daughter was ecstatic, too. Irene said the expression on her daughter's face was priceless; she'd only ever known her mother to be sick in bed and unable to do anything.

God is great!

Become Active in the Supernatural

I want to share with you practical ways to step into supernatural ministry and begin walking in a new measure of signs, wonders, and miracles.

The first way has much to do with the subtitle of this book. You actually have to *surrender* to *significance*. You have to quit "trying" to do things in your own strength. Instead you must realize that God is the only One who can bring fruit through your efforts. You have to quit wondering whether you are "special" enough or "good" enough for God to use you or whether you have the right type of formula to produce supernatural results. Establish in your thoughts once and for all that *He has chosen you to do the works of Jesus.* Period. Follow Him just like He followed His Father, and you will do the works!

Here's some further insight:

1. Totally immerse yourself in the river of God. I am referring to the prophetic encounter described in Ezekiel 47, where the angel of the Lord led Ezekiel into the river of God until the river was so deep that he could not cross it. *"He measured off another thousand, but now it was a river that I could not cross, because the water had risen and was deep enough to swim in—a river that no one could cross"* (Ezek. 47:5 NIV).

   The river represents the Holy Spirit and our allowing Him to have total control over our lives and ministries. When the river is ankle deep, you can still walk out; you still have control. When the water is up to your knees, it is deeper, but you can still wade out of the river. When the river is up to your waist, it is harder to wade through its currents, but you can; you are still in control.

   But Ezekiel describes how the angel brought him to such depths that he could not cross over the waters. That is the place God wants us to be—the place of total surrender to the Holy Spirit, the place where God is in control in every area of our lives. When the Holy Spirit is welcomed and hosted in this way, He begins to manifest Himself in power.

   The river is so powerful that the trees lined up along its banks provide fruit for food and healing in their leaves. *"Fruit trees of all kinds will grow on both banks of the river. Their leaves will not wither, nor will their fruit fail. Every month they will bear, because the water from the sanctuary flows to them. Their fruit will serve for food and their leaves for healing"* (Ezek. 47:12 NIV).

   Luke 5:17 also assures us that when Jesus ministered *"the power of the Lord was present for Him to heal the sick."* Is the power of the Lord present in your life, in your home, and in your church? Get in the river of God and stay in the river of God. Plunge yourself into its waters spiritually, physically, and mentally. When you do, the Lord can do marvelous things. Bring others with you.

2. Contend for supernatural healing. When I say *contend,* I mean that I want you to be like Jacob; he would not let go of the angel until the angel blessed him. (See Genesis 32:22-29.) We have followed Bill Johnson's apostolic decree that his church will be a "cancer-free zone." I have made a similar decree, and we have seen remarkable results. By contending, I am talking about being in faith and fighting the unseen spiritual war so God can supernaturally heal the sick.

3. Walk in faith that God wants *every believer* equipped for the work of ministry (see Eph. 4:11-12). Bishop Bill Hamon calls this the "Day of the Saints."[3]

As I have often said, we cannot reach the world's one billion plus Muslims unless *every believer* is used by God to advance His Kingdom. God wants to use every believer to heal the sick, cast out demons, and raise the dead (see Matt. 10:7; Mark 16:17-18). Every believer has been given extraordinary authority by our Lord Jesus (see Luke 10:19; Matt 28:18-19).

The fact of the matter is that the least in the Kingdom is greater than John the Baptist (see Matt. 11:11), and John was the greatest of all the prophets in the Old Covenant! He was greater than Elisha who raised the dead; he was greater than Moses or Elijah who moved in extraordinary signs and wonders. We simply need to know who our God is and who we are in Christ.

Winkie Pratney, a world-renowned minister, speaker, and writer—and one of my best friends—shared with me a true story that illustrates my last point.

A married couple Winkie knew in the suburbs of Kansas City was going through a marital crisis. To alleviate the stress of the marriage, the wife went out for a jog. She noticed a man standing in the corn field as she jogged by. They made eye contact but didn't say anything to each other.

After jogging a few miles, she turned around to go home and saw the same man standing in the cornfield. This time he said something to her. He said, "Don't you know who *I* am? Don't you know who *you* are? When you know these two things, nothing will be too difficult for you."

With those words, the man disappeared in front of her eyes. She realized that Jesus had appeared to her.

Yes, you are significant!

Endnotes

1. Ché Ahn, *Into The Fire* (Ventura, CA: Regal Books, 1998), 78-81.

2. *Ibid.,* 85-86.

3. Bill Hamon, *The Day of The Saints: Equipping Believers for their Revolutionary Role in Ministry* (Shippensburg, PA: Destiny Image, 2005).

CHAPTER 6

Reaching the Lost Through Signs and Wonders

Seeing the power of God through revival has given me a whole new perspective about the power of God to save souls. Akiko is just one reason I will never evangelize as I did before.

An Unbeliever's Power Encounter

Akiko came reluctantly to one of our services. A young Japanese woman, she had been invited by another Japanese student. Her friend was studying at nearby Fuller Theological Seminary and had experienced a powerful encounter with the Lord just days earlier. While visiting Mott Auditorium, he was filled with the Holy Spirit and began speaking in tongues (see Acts 2:4)—much to his surprise! He had previously enjoyed mocking Charismatics and was the last person he would have expected to become one!

When I first saw Akiko after the service, I remember asking her if she spoke English. "A little," she replied. I asked her if she wanted to accept Jesus into her heart. Hesitating briefly, she answered, "No, I cannot. My father is a Shinto. My mother is a Buddhist."

I told her I understood. Having visited Japan and having many internationals as friends, I knew that the number of Christians in Japan was less than one percent. One reason is that Japanese people are expected to conform readily to the norms of their society. Obviously, becoming a Christian is contrary to the norm. It is so serious that doing so would mean having to renounce the heritage of one's family and culture.

The Japanese have a saying: "If a nail is sticking up, it has to be hammered down." So when Akiko said she could not become a Christian because her parents were not Christians, I understood. I asked if I could pray a blessing upon her anyway; she said "Yes." Although many Japanese may never receive Christ, they are among the most polite people I know and will usually welcome your prayers. God loves the opportunity, and He will do the work even if it seems nothing more than a formality!

When ministering to Japanese people, I find it's best to offer a simple, gentle prayer. When I prayed for Akiko, I simply asked the Holy Spirit to give her a revelation of Jesus (see Eph. 1:17). As soon as the words left my mouth, the Holy Spirit fell on her. She slumped to the floor and remained there for 20 minutes. I had seen many people fall under the Spirit's power before, but to the best of my knowledge, they were already Christians. I remember thinking, *Isn't this interesting? Here is an unbelieving Japanese person resting (slain) in the Spirit.*

Akiko remained resting in the Lord's presence for quite some time. After a while, I became concerned; she remained there and hadn't moved an inch. I eventually came back to her, got down on my knees, and asked her if she was OK. She nodded her head in affirmation.

"Akiko, did Jesus reveal Himself to you?" I asked.

She nodded up and down again. I could tell by looking at her that she was full of the presence of God, so much so that I knew I could ask her about salvation again. "Would you like to invite Jesus into your heart and become a follower of His?" I asked.

Akiko nodded *Yes!* I helped her up to a sitting position. We prayed the sinner's prayer and Akiko became a beautiful Christian. Since then she has grown in her commitment to the Lord in spite of the opposition by her family.

The lesson I learned was this: I could have talked to Akiko until I was blue in the face. I could have shared all my best apologetics about how Jesus is superior to Buddha. I could have spoken with great fervor and insight—but most likely it would not have changed her mind about Jesus.

If I had shared that way by mere natural insight, Akiko might have prayed the prayer with me because she felt pressured or wanted to be polite. However, I doubt that she truly would have given her heart to the Lord. Yet, when she experienced the love, the presence, and the power of the Holy Spirit firsthand, her heart was opened, and she responded with all the sincerity within her. There was no hesitation in Akiko, and you could tell that her enthusiastic response was the work of God and not man.

Changing My Evangelism Philosophy

This experience has changed my whole philosophy of evangelism. Before my encounter with Akiko, I would simply present the Gospel and allow the person to either accept or reject Christ. It was fairly black and white for me, and I was pretty matter of fact about it. After all, we are all sinners and salvation is what God offers.

Now I realize there is no comparison between an unbeliever's "unassisted" encounter with the matchless reality of the Holy Spirit and my attempts to lead them to Christ. This idea gives me a whole new insight into *power evangelism,* a term popularized by the late John Wimber. John led the Vineyard denomination and did much to equip Christians for sharing the reality of the Gospel more effectively. This reality was demonstrated, not only through the sharing of the facts about salvation, but also through the signs and wonders which followed.

This was the same method used by Jesus and the apostle Paul. Paul made it clear that he did not come to us with *"persuasive words of human wisdom, but in demonstration of the Spirit and of power"* (1 Cor. 2:4).

God always expected the power of the Holy Spirit to be involved in conversion. That is why He gave the Spirit to us. I believe we are "filled with the Spirit" for our own edification and growth, and I believe the Spirit comes "upon us" to reach out and impact the lives of others.

In short, power evangelism takes place when an unbeliever sees and experiences the power of God in a mighty way (such as through miracles or healings) and receives a rational presentation of the Gospel.[1] C. Peter Wagner unapologetically says, "Across the board, the most effective evangelism in today's world is accompanied by manifestations of supernatural power."[2] I personally believe that the primary expansion of Christianity in the early Church came as a result of power evangelism. It is not new—it is just far rarer than it needs to be.

Although I love all kinds of evangelism and I admire anyone who is devoted to this great cause, I believe the most effective demonstration of salvation we can offer anywhere on the planet comes through this kind of power encounter. There is no question in my mind that such demonstrations—which are as old as the Bible—are also on the cutting edge of what the Holy Spirit is saying concerning evangelism today.

Again and again, we observe people believing the Gospel *after* experiencing signs and wonders. Just look at the book of Acts! Spiritual scales are removed from the eyes of unbelievers as they experience or witness the power of God. Second Corinthians 4:4 says, *"The god of this age has blinded the minds of unbelievers, so that they cannot see the light of the gospel..."* (NIV). When unbelievers experience healings or see miracles such as occurred in the city of Samaria through Philip and Peter (see Acts 8), their spiritual eyes are opened and salvation occurs!

Still, I had a problem. My problem was that I had underestimated the forms which power evangelism could take. I thought the only people exposed to power evangelism were those who directly saw or experienced miracles or healings. I began to realize, however, that non-Christians could experience the presence and the power of the Holy Spirit in other ways that opened their hearts to the Gospel just as effectively. I found that all I had to do was to ask the Holy Spirit to touch them or to reveal Jesus to them. The anointing did the rest.

Just as in our own salvation, it doesn't depend on our "goodness" or works or having some "huge ministry" or "call." It is all a gift, anyway. God so desires to see all come to the knowledge of Him that He will honor our requests for Him to manifest Himself to the unbeliever through the Holy Spirit—if we simply ask in faith.

Binding the Powers of Darkness

Here's another illustration of my point. Two high school summer exchange students (also from Japan) came to our Sunday church service. As practicing Buddhists, they had never been to a Christian church. Their American host was a member of Harvest Rock Church and decided to bring them along for Sunday worship.

I had an opportunity to meet these two young girls and their host before the service began. I encouraged the host to bring the students to the front of the church at the end of the service during our time of personal ministry. I knew that any encounter they could have with the Holy Spirit was likely to cause them to be more open to the Gospel, and I didn't want them to miss the opportunity.

At the end of the service, I saw the host and the two girls coming toward me. Through Yoshi, a Japanese church member and interpreter, I asked if I could pray for them. They both nodded. I wasn't concerned about whether they were just being polite. Here's why: as I began to pray, the Holy Spirit began to fall on them. They both started to sway, one more so than the other.

I began to discern some strong demonic hindrances, so I asked through Yoshi about their religious background. At this time I heard from their own mouths that they were Buddhists. Because satan blinds the eyes of the unbelieving, I was led in this particular situation to bind the powers of darkness that were hindering these two from receiving

Jesus (see Matt. 16:19; 18:18). Then I began to pray that God would reveal His love to each of them.

I clearly saw that they were being mightily overshadowed by the presence of the Holy Spirit (see Luke 1:35; 9:34). I briefly proceeded to share with them how Jesus had died for them and asked if they would like to receive Jesus into their hearts. They both said "Yes," and became Christians!

Although they didn't fall under the power of the Holy Spirit before the prayer of salvation as Akiko had, one fell after accepting Christ. As each one personally experienced the power and presence of the Holy Spirit, however, the Gospel became real to them. When they heard the explanation of salvation, their hearts were already turned to Christ!

Sharing the Truth of the Gospel

I want to state emphatically that the truth of the Gospel must be shared clearly in words as well, but I believe it can be better received by those who first experience the power of the Holy Spirit.

My theory is that such a power encounter with the Lord pulls down the spiritual forces that hinder the person from coming to Christ in the first place. Then the love of God is revealed. Paul says that *"the kindness of God leads* [us] *to repentance..."* (Rom. 2:4 NASB). What better way is there to experience the kindness of God than to feel it! Surely it is better felt than taught!

In the very first year of the revival at Harvest Rock, I saw perhaps 50 people in our church alone come to the Lord—people who would traditionally be considered difficult to reach (such as the Japanese and Chinese Buddhists). Yet when I simply laid my hands on their heads and praying for the Holy Spirit to come and reveal Jesus, things changed. In the years that have passed, that number has now become thousands around the globe. That shows how mightily God can work through just one person!

Power Evangelism Is Getting the Job Done

Many ministries have followed in that path. Perhaps one of the more recently known is that of Rolland and Heidi Baker and Iris Ministries. For some years, they ministered in their own self-effort with few results. Heidi, with a Doctorate in Systematic Theology, was perhaps the most frustrated of the two. Upon hearing of the renewal/revival in Toronto, she and Rolland went there to experience more of God.

Once there, Heidi had an incredible encounter with the Lord. It changed her life forever. She was overcome by the Spirit and the weighty presence of God—"glued" to the floor, if you will, for seven days and nights. She and her Rolland were completely transformed.

Since they returned to their budding ministry in Mozambique, the power of God has become the norm in everything they do. They simply load up their tiny old pick-up truck with the *Jesus Video* and go out in search of new villagers who will come to view it. Then they invite the sick, blind, and even the dead to be brought forth and healed.

God begins moving and villages get saved. I have personally taken teams to Mozambique to partner with Rolland and Heidi, practically on an annual basis since 2006. One time, Sue and I went into the bush with Heidi and her team and ministered at a remote village. We held a powerful deliverance service where demons were cast out of most of the villagers, including the chief and the witch doctor. To say the least, when the chief and the witch doctor gave their lives to Jesus, the whole village came to know Christ! A church was established in the village.

We entered the village terrified of being stoned by the Muslims who lived there. However, we left as heroes; instead of stoning us, they lavished us with vegetables from their village garden. In just a few short years following more than 20 years of virtual fruitlessness, Heidi and Rolland now have more than 8,000 churches. They feed thousands upon thousands every day, and they care for thousands of orphans in their orphanages. They have ministries all over Africa and are expanding to India and elsewhere. It is a wildfire move of the love of God like nothing else I have ever seen!

Laughing Revival

The toughest circumstances can be changed by praying for the Holy Spirit's touch—as my next story demonstrates. It doesn't have to be a physical healing or miraculous deliverance from a wheelchair. It can be a powerful touch of the heart.

Lisa was emotionally distant. She was a 15-year-old Korean-American teenager who grew up alongside gang-member friends in the Las Vegas area. She had been shot at twice. One time she ducked at the last second and a bullet flew right over her head. Her mother didn't know what to do with her, so she sent her to live with her aunt in Seattle, Washington. I recall when her aunt shared with me in exasperation and desperation how out of control Lisa's life had become. Lisa was rebellious, a crack addict, and wasting away on drugs and gangster rap music. I told her to bring Lisa to my evening ministry appointment.

That evening I was scheduled to speak to a small group of Korean Christians. When Lisa came in, you couldn't miss her. She stood out like a sore thumb. There she was in her baggy, gang-style clothing. A dark shadow seemed to veil her hardened face. She didn't look 15; she looked like a burned-out adult.

Lisa was the only non-Christian at this gathering. During my message, I was continually conscious of her. In all honesty, I was preaching to Lisa and hoping she would respond to the altar call I was planning to give at the end of the service.

I gave the altar call, but Lisa didn't respond. Afterward we had a time of ministry. I began to pray for people to be filled with the Holy Spirit. People were falling to the ground as the Holy Spirit rested on them. They were "manifesting" or showing signs of God's presence on them by shaking or trembling or both.

I wondered what was going through Lisa's mind during all of this. I decided to go over to her. After introducing myself and chatting for a moment, I simply asked Lisa if she would like to give her life to Jesus. She told me she wasn't ready yet. I said I appreciated her honest answer, but asked if she would mind if I prayed for her anyway. "Do whatever you want," she said indifferently. She seemed bored and ready to bolt at the earliest opportunity. Not wanting to crowd her or add to her discomfort, I stood several feet away as I prayed: "Jesus, please reveal to Lisa how much You love her," I asked quietly.

As soon as I said those words, Lisa started to laugh. At first, I wondered if she was laughing at me or at what I had prayed. I soon saw that she was trying not to laugh as she made a futile effort to cover her mouth with her hands. That is when I knew this laughter was the Holy Spirit flooding her!

Many have called this manifestation of God a "laughing revival" because people laugh uncontrollably when the Holy Spirit fills them with unspeakable joy. When I realized this was happening to Lisa, I said to her, "Don't fight the laughter. The Holy Spirit is revealing Himself to you!"

John Arnott had always encouraged us to "bless what the Father is doing" when we saw the Holy Spirit on someone, especially in an unusual or unexpected way. At this point, I went near Lisa to bless her and ask the Father to do more. As soon as I lifted my hands, she fell to the floor speaking in tongues. This amazed me. I hadn't yet led her to the Lord, nor had we prayed the sinner's prayer. In fact, Lisa had just said that she wasn't ready to come to Christ!

I asked the Lord to give me Scripture concerning what I was witnessing. Immediately, Acts 10 came to my mind. As Peter was preaching to the house of Cornelius, the Holy Spirit fell, and all of the members of the household began to speak in tongues. Apparently, God, who knows the hearts of people, knew that Lisa had changed her mind once she experienced that initial touch of the Spirit in laughter. She then was converted and filled with the Holy Spirit all at the same time! And all without my help!

Lisa stayed on the floor for almost two hours, still speaking in tongues and shaking under the power of the Spirit. Everyone had gone home except a few people, including Lisa and her aunt. I needed to be going, so I leaned over and told her it was time to go home.

"I can't move. I can't get up," she replied. "There are too many... too many!"

I thought she was saying she was seeing too many demons, which meant that I would have another late night ministering deliverance. "There are too many what?" I queried.

"Too many faces!" she answered. "Faces of whom?" I asked. "Faces of my friends. Their faces have been flashing before me all night," came the reply.

Her answer hit me with tremendous force. Not only did God save her, fill her with His Spirit, and give her a prayer language, but He also gave her the spirit of intercession! For almost two hours, that is what Lisa had been doing. She had been praying for her gang-member friends!

God gave me important insight from His heart that night: this next generation is vital to Him, and intercession is such a key part of their revival that God wants to save and recruit young people on the spot just as He did Lisa. *There is no time to lose as they cry out for their perishing friends! We simply must be conduits and give the Holy Spirit the opportunity He needs to reach them.*

Lisa stayed on the floor unable to move for the next eight hours. Not wanting to disturb what the Holy Spirit had begun, we left her in the safe care of our attendants. When I saw her the next day, I hardly recognized her. She was radiant. She looked soft; she looked like a 15-year-old. God had erased so much of her hard life in so little time. It was incredible.

We baptized Lisa. To this day, she is a transformed young lady.

Power evangelism works. The key to this power is prayer, extraordinary prayer. This is another truth of renewal in which I found myself growing more than at any other time of my life.

Endnotes

1. John Wimber and Kevin Springer, *Power Evangelism,* 2nd ed. (San Francisco: HarperSanFrancisco, 1992), 35.

2. C. Peter Wagner, *The Third Wave of the Holy Spirit* (Ann Arbor: Servant Publications, 1988), 87.

CHAPTER 7

Driven by Prayer: A Paradigm Shift

One of the greatest keys to bringing God's will to the earth is prayer.

Billy Graham once said there are three keys to his crusades: Prayer. Prayer. And prayer.[1] John Wesley asserted, "God does nothing on earth save in answer to believing prayer.[2]

I couldn't agree more.

All that I have been sharing about what God has done at Harvest Rock Church is a direct result of prayer. Every story I will yet reveal in this book has the same basis. Prayer is one way we give over to God what is rightfully His: results!

I have actually heard some people say that the renewal which has been apparent since the mid-1990s hit the world sovereignly, without prayer. I understand why people might say this. The Toronto group, for example, had not held any unusual prayer sessions before the Holy Spirit fell on January 20, 1994. To my knowledge, neither had the Anaheim Vineyard.

I believe, however, the Holy Spirit always falls in answer to prayer. I agree with what one leader said: "There has never been a historic revival without extraordinary prayer." These visitations of the last 15 or more years are most likely a result of all the fervent prayers the Body of Christ offered during the 1980s and early 1990s.

Although the Church as a whole did not see much fruit during the decade preceding the outpouring, one thing it did do was pray. The same was true for us. At least we prayed, especially my friend Lou Engle.

An Incomparable Intercessor

My mentor and professor, Dr. C. Peter Wagner, once said that if he were going to plant a church, the first person he would recruit would be an intercessor.

By God's grace, I did not need to recruit one. God had already joined me with Lou Engle, an incomparable intercessor. Lou is far more than a prayer warrior who oversees intercession in our church. He has been a loyal friend, confidante, and prophet—to me, Harvest Rock Church, and the apostolic network I am privileged to lead (Harvest International Ministry).

In fact, Lou reminds me of Frank Bartleman, a revivalist who gave himself to fasting and prayer during the Azusa Street Revival in 1906. I have never met anyone who embodies and personifies prayer as does Lou Engle. In fact, that very DNA is what led him to father TheCall. This innovative outreach has now become a worldwide prayer movement to tear down the wicked strongholds of society and to contend for global revival. Many tangible, life-changing results can be attributed directly to the events or "Calls" held all over the world. The story of TheCall will be detailed in a later chapter.

Extraordinary Prayer

Renowned 18th-century theologian Jonathan Edwards said that if you want to experience revival, there must be "explicit agreement, visible union and extraordinary prayer."[3]

A trail of such prayer pervades the accounts of what has happened at Harvest Rock Church. Persistence has borne results: as Alice Smith puts it today, "Pray until something happens."[4]

When we began Harvest Rock Church, we started as a prayer meeting. When we heard from God to go into protracted revival meetings, we began the first 21 days with praying and fasting. That was the first time I had been on a 21-day liquid fast. We met five days a week for prayer, and in the evenings we had revival meetings.

It is hard to believe that during the decade of the 1990s we hosted one of the longest revival meetings in the world. Toronto Airport Christian Fellowship and Brownsville Assemblies of God hosted similar revivals as well—along with more short-lived "hot spots" comparable to the most recent Lakeland Revival and other "zones" found around the globe.

I firmly believe that the enduring quality of our revival stems from the fact that we devote, dedicate, and sustain the meetings through prayer.

Continuous Prayer

A key development in the life of our church came in the fall of 1995. The Lord began to impress upon Lou Engle that we should establish a Twenty-Four-Hour House of Prayer for All Nations. For years, Lou wanted to establish this kind of sustained prayer, but the timing wasn't right. Now, the Lord was giving us permission to do it.

We held a meeting of handpicked intercessors and shared the vision of holding around-the-clock prayer at Mott. Each day was divided into three-hour shifts from which intercessors could select a single three-hour shift each week. They committed to whatever timeslot they chose and could invite anyone they desired to join them in prayer during that time.

Lou was also inspired to create a clear job description and outline of what needed to be covered during each shift. A special room was devoted exclusively to continual prayer. It contained a map of the world covering a full wall. The carpet was extra thick, with kneeling rails, pillows, and a variety of chairs. The shelves were filled with quality testimonies and materials about prayer and world missions.

New journals were regularly placed in the room to cover current prayer requests and answers; record prophecies, revelations, and dreams; and list the names of those from our midst who are involved in ministry around the world. A wide selection of praise and worship music and a small stereo completed the simple furnishings.

During each session, there would be intimate worship and praise, as well as many styles of prayer covering many topics as the Spirit led.

To inaugurate the prayer room, we decided to call our church to an extended time of praying and fasting for the first 40 days of 1996. During this time, Lou personally baptized the room by praying and fasting for 40 days. For the final ten days of his fast, Lou literally lived in the prayer room, praying without ceasing. He only left to walk across the street to his home to shower and change clothes.

After the 40 days were completed, prayer shifts began in earnest. We cried out for our missionaries; we pled for nations; we made declarations over Hollywood and the youth of our country; we interceded for the government; and invoked the Lord for revival. There was no end to all that was prayed and is still being prayed.

Some would literally place their hands on the map covering the wall and pray for different nations. Others would weep and whisper in tongues. Some shifts were like a military drill, with the directives of God being "issued" in the Spirit realm. It was new for us to have such intensive prayer going forth at all times. But as we have seen, it is where the Lord is inviting many to participate.

We now find that throughout the world, the Lord is prompting perhaps thousands of ministries to host 24/7 prayer, 24/7 worship to the Lord, or both. As we find ourselves in these last days, God is glorifying His name day and night throughout the whole earth. As the prayers rise as incense before God's altar through the conduits of those who will give themselves to prayer and worship, I have no doubt the atmosphere of the earth is being changed into the atmosphere of Heaven

I don't know where we would be as a church, where Harvest International would be as a ministry, or where our staff would be as leaders if the intercessors had not given and did not continue to give of themselves in prayer. I believe intercessors are one of the most critical positions of honor and value in God's Kingdom, and I want to thank again every person who has been involved with us in prayer over the years. You are truly Kingdom builders, and your reward will be abundant in Heaven! (See Matthew 6:33.)

As Rick Joyner wrote of his vision of Heaven:

Those closest to the throne of God were those who gave themselves to intercession on earth....As I approached the Judgment Seat of Christ, those in the highest ranks were also sitting on thrones that were all a part of His throne...it seemed that faithful, praying women and mothers occupied more thrones than any other single group.[5]

I believe this is so. Many people feel they don't have a "full-time ministry," but we all do—it is never ceasing to pray. Some of the most faithful with this mandate throughout the ages have been mothers and grandmothers to whom prayer is continuous as they go about raising the next godly generation. God asks us to *"give Him no rest till He establishes Jerusalem and makes her the praise of the earth"* (Isa. 62:7 NIV). We are all included in that directive.

The Moravians, unparalleled reformers and catalysts of revival and missions centuries ago, held continuous prayer sessions for more than 100 years. We would like to experience continuous prayer until the Lord returns. It may take on various forms and timelines over the years, but until the Kingdom is preached to all nations, we shall not cease to live a lifestyle of fasting and prayer (see Matt. 24:14).

Although not everyone is called to establish a Twenty-Four-Hour House of Prayer for All Nations, we can all do something. Perhaps 24/7 prayer can be done for a season, with church members signing up for time slots and praying from home so that all hours of the day are covered. God has led many churches to sponsor a weekly all-night prayer meeting. Surely regular corporate prayer meetings are vital. Some have joined with other churches (one group has more than 25 churches citywide) to have 24-hour worship and prayer for the city.

The important thing is to do what you believe the Father is showing you to do in regard to prayer and to "follow the cloud" as He leads you.

Forty Days of Prayer and Fasting

Lou Engle "takes the cake" (a poor analogy, perhaps) for completing the most 40-day fasts of any man I know. I jokingly say that I originally hired Lou to be on staff to do the fasting while I do the eating. Since Lou has recently moved out from our direct staff to his own wider ministry, the local prayer and fasting ball is now squarely back in my court.

Quite frankly, I really do not like to fast. In fact, I used to think I didn't need to fast. My wife Sue (one of the pastors of Harvest Rock Church) is another person who has given herself to prayer and fasting. I had reasoned that between Sue and Lou's dedication the whole church and I were covered, but I was wrong.

In the latter part of 1996, God began to confront me about an extended fast. Like many people, I had read Bill Bright's book about fasting, *The Coming Revival.* In it, Bright contends:

> The power of fasting as it relates to prayer is the spiritual atomic bomb of our moment in history to bring down the strongholds of evil, bring a great revival and spiritual awakening to America, and accelerate the fulfillment of the Great Commission.[6]

The second thing that God began to do was convict through the writings of C. Peter Wagner on prayer. He wrote a six-volume series called *The Prayer Warrior Series.* His most recent book on prayer, *Praying with Power,* sums up the point that convinced me that I could not just rely on Lou or Sue. Instead, as the Senior Pastor of Harvest Rock, I had to lead.

> If the church is ever to become a house of prayer, the senior pastor must cast the vision and assume the leadership of the church's prayer ministry. That does not mean that the pastor cannot delegate the administration and the implementation of the prayer ministry…all the church members should know without question that their pastor has prioritized prayer in his or her personal life and ministry.[7]

Today, I couldn't agree more with Peter. The Lord began to speak to me that we as a pastoral staff should go on a 40-day fast together in 1997. We had heard about the pastors and churches in Houston fasting the last 40 days of 1996. The fast was led by city leader Doug Stringer of Someone Cares Houston. (You know it *must* be God's doing when people fast through Thanksgiving and Christmas!) John Arnott had also shared with me that his church in Toronto was planning a corporate fast the first 40 days of 1997. I heard that some 50 pastors and their churches in Dallas were planning to do the same thing. We decided our fast would begin one week after Lent and culminate 40 days later, on Easter Sunday.

That January, I shared the idea with the church, noting that we were committed to the fast as a pastoral staff and anyone who so desired could join us. To my amazement, more than 600 people made a commitment to participate in the fast in some way. Many people went on a vegetable fast, others ate one meal a day, and so on. More than 65 people engaged in a liquid fast for the entire 40 days. I was one of them.

Initially, I had a hard time. I was used to drinking diet Coke, so for the first three days I suffered caffeine withdrawal and experienced headaches and fatigue. The second week I started to dream of food almost nightly. I remember one dream very well: I came home and I saw a bowl of rice and a plate of Korean barbecue on the table. The dream seemed so real. I sat down and devoured the food. Then I realized I had broken my fast. I felt terrible about it. I felt like Esau who had given over his birthright for some measly food. Then I realized there was nothing I could do because I had already broken the fast, so I decided I should eat more. I had another helping. When I woke up, I realized it was only a dream. I was so grateful!

I think the dream motivated me and helped me not to break the fast even when I was tempted to do so. There is one practical note I would like to share concerning extended fasting: I was losing more muscle mass than body fat. After ten days, a physician in our church warned me to drink some liquid protein and to do some light exercise. That was vital advice for my health. Soon I began to lose body fat and not muscle. Use wisdom and consider *your* physician's advice about fasting. This is an especially important tip for those who regularly engage in extended fasts to maintain their body health. Of course, if the Lord has clearly spoken to you differently, follow His lead.

Even though most people lose weight fasting, that is not the reason for the fast. My main goal was to grow in love—a prayer that God is still answering in many wonderful ways which I will yet share with you in the pages of this book.

We concluded the 40 days of fasting by conducting a healing conference. Mahesh Chavda was invited to be with us. On Friday night, he led us in a "prayer watch," which is essentially an all-night prayer meeting. Around three in the morning, a most unusual thing happened. A huge tree in front of the auditorium split in half, as if struck by lightning. It happened to be right in front of my parking place! There was no wind, no rain, no lightning or any other natural cause for such an occurrence!

Someone who was leaving the prayer meeting reported what happened. When I shared it with Mahesh, he thought it was a sign that demonic strongholds at Mott were broken and that we would now see a greater release of the Holy Spirit. Mahesh had witnessed this kind of thing several times during his crusades in Africa. He told us that many times God would break the spirit of witchcraft by splitting a tree, usually by lightning. Most often, that particular tree was known to the local witches as a power source. Whether that applies to this particular incident or not, I do believe God was giving us a sign to encourage us that we were right on track through our obedience in fasting and prayer. It is filled with power! As many who fast say, the results are seldom seen during the fast, but quite often seen after you are finished. Don't give up, and don't look with your natural eyes for the results. You are changing the spiritual climate!

The Fruit of Prayer

Most likely, none of us will know the full effect of our intercession in this life until we get to Heaven. We do, however, know of several things that happened in our city that we believe were influenced greatly by our prayers and that of many others in the days and months which followed this first extended fast of Harvest Rock Church.

One was a dramatic name change for an important public landmark. Lou Engle gives this account of what happened:

> Protecting the original water source of Pasadena and Los Angeles is a dam bearing the name of Devil's Gate. My fellow intercessors and I sensed strongly that such a name literally brought a curse on the city.
>
> A 1947 local newspaper article said, "It's true Devil's Gate is named because of the resemblance of the rocks to his satanic majesty." One night, I awoke from a dream with these words spoken to me: "Go and pour the salt of your purity on it." I didn't know what this word pertained to at that moment, but prior to coming to Pasadena, the Lord had given me a word from the passage where Elisha poured salt into the water source of Jericho and healed the contaminated waters (see 2 Kings 2:19-22).
>
> That morning in a prayer meeting, an intercessor in our church prayed that God would change the name of Devil's Gate. Then it struck me with much force to go and pour salt into the stream at Devil's Gate as an act of prophetic intercession—and ask the Lord to change the name, break the curse, and let the rivers of revival flow bringing fruitfulness to the Los Angeles Valley. We

took our Greater Pasadena for Christ intercession team to the dam and did precisely that. At that time, Southern California had been experiencing a severe drought of five years' duration. I know thousands of other Californians were praying for rain as well, but God encouraged us when eight days later it began to rain. The rains were so heavy the newspapers called it a "Miracle March." It was astonishing. We pondered this. Could it be a sign of renewal and revival—first the natural, then the spiritual?

However, for two years, the name of the dam remained the same. One of our intercessors went to God to inquire again. He spoke to her that the name would be changed, and it would be an Indian name. Soon after, a *Los Angeles Times* newspaper article added to our excitement of answered prayer when it spoke of a name change for the dam: Haha-mongna. That's the name the Gabrielinos (early Pasadena Indians) gave to what now is known as Devil's Gate, the 250-acre area at the north end of the Arroyo Seco. ... The English language translation is "Flowing Waters: Fruitful Valley." Nearly everyone agrees that Hahamongna will be a more appropriate name for this long-neglected community asset after it is restored to its natural state....

"Flowing rivers and a fruitful valley"—that is our intercession now, and what has begun since the outpouring began in 1994.[8]

Another major turnaround we witnessed in our city was the repentance and conversion of a major cult. Many people have no doubt heard of the Worldwide Church of God (WCG) or its magazine *The Plain Truth*. In the early days of their being headquartered in Pasadena, we believed they were a major demonic stronghold in our city, and we repeatedly prayed and lifted them up.

I am not saying we were the reason the WCG changed, but we may have played a part. God had been working on the organization for quite some time. I know many former members who had become Christians and were fervently interceding for WCG. I do believe, however, the many collective prayers, including ours, were responsible for a radical transformation.

I remember hearing Jack Hayford say, "To my knowledge, never has a cult turned around so dramatically in the history of Christianity." Today, the WCG is a member of the National Association of Evangelicals. I now know many of the leaders personally, including Joseph Tkach, the president of the WCG. I honestly can say they are true brothers in Christ. (If God can bring down the walls of deception of the WCG through the prayers of the saints, then we need to be earnest in faith and prayer that the scales of deception also fall from groups such as the Mormons and the Muslims.)

It never occurred to me how WCG would come back around into my life again just a few years later. As realigning took place throughout the Worldwide Church of God, they decided they would no longer maintain their world headquarters campus in downtown Pasadena. Their auditorium, called the "Crown Jewel" of the city, was offered by special private sale—to us!

The home of Harvest Rock Church is now in the Ambassador Auditorium—an incredible miracle that takes a whole exciting chapter to share later in this book!

Persevering in Prayer

I am ever so grateful about what the Lord has done in bringing renewal to our city. I believe the extended duration of this visitation added to the impact it has had upon multiplied thousands over the years has made it into a revival. The full impact of the revival is not yet seen, but I believe it is coming.

There is a temptation to lose our fervency in prayer when things seem to be happening sovereignly. Instead, we have learned that when God pours out His unmerited grace, we should give ourselves to prayer as never before (see 1 Thess. 5:17). We need to give God no rest until multitudes are swept into the Kingdom and a radical transformation is seen in all areas of society.

As we receive this new strengthening and vision, we are beginning to slowly see more amazing and widespread change throughout the nations. God is raising up wise strategists such as Lance Wallnau and others to unfold how we can influence every "mountain of culture" by taking our place as believers and serving at the top of each mountain. The mountains include education, government, media, the economy, religion, arts and entertainment, and family. This takes revival from salvation alone to societal transformation—the destination I am sure our King of all governments intends.

There is a further step beyond societal transformation: I believe this "final" goal is *reformation*. This is where we pray, work, infiltrate, and influence society until there is a firm infrastructure built to sustain God's values for the long term and cause them to replace man's "good ideas." As Alice Smith says in her book *Beyond the Veil,* "Burning, believing, prevailing, persuading, persevering, intimate prayer always precedes a move of God."[9]

To this end we continue to labor, pray, and believe! We must press forth until He makes His people a praise on the earth...and all of the kingdoms of this world have become the kingdoms of Christ! (See Revelation 11:15.)

Endnotes

1. Ché Ahn, *Fire Evangelism* (Grand Rapids, MI: Chosen Books, 2006), 107.

2. Dutch Sheets, *Intercessory Prayer* (Ventura, CA: Regal Books, 1996), 23.

3. "A Humble Attempt to Promote Explicit Agreement and Visible Union of God's People, in Extraordinary Prayer, for the Revival of Religion and the Advancement of Christ's Kingdom on Earth," The Works of Jonathan Edwards, vol. 2, from

Christian Classic Ethereal Library http://www.ccel.org/ccel/edwards/works2.viii.html?highlight=visible,union,and, extraordinary,prayer#highlight (accessed March 19, 2009).

4. Alice Smith, *Beyond the Veil* (Ventura, CA: Renew Books, 1997), 39.

5. Rick Joyner, *The Final Quest* (New Kensington, PA: Whitaker House, 1996), 116-117.

6. Bill Bright, *The Coming Revival* (Orlando: New Life Publications, 1995), 16.

7. C. Peter Wagner, *Praying with Power* (Shippensburg, PA: Destiny Image, 1997), 148-149.

8. Ché Ahn, *Into The Fire* (Ventura, CA: Renew Books, 1998), 104-105.

9. Smith, 2.

CHAPTER 8

How Far Will Your Heart Take You?

True revival brings permanent and wonderful change in the lives of those who experience it. It goes past the walls of the church or the mood of a city or even one's salvation to transform those who partake of it.

Little did I know that perhaps the greatest change—the call to wholeness and holiness—could come through the love and laughter the Father has been pouring out so graciously for more than 15 years. I believe God is refreshing and healing His own sons and daughters so they can usher in the sweeping worldwide revival that is yet to come.

We know that inside every believer is a desire to walk holy with the Lord. Yet all of us struggle greatly in our quest for victory over sin. Granted, holiness is a process, a truth that should set us free and release us from the condemnation that undermines our efforts to live His way. Wonderfully, however, I have grasped and experienced truths in this renewal that have enabled me to leap forward with tremendous strides in my personal endeavors toward this goal.

The greatest revelation I have received is that holiness has everything to do with love. We cannot be holy without first receiving His love. Again, it is God's initiative toward us—even as was our salvation. God promises in Ezekiel 11:19-20: *"I will give them an undivided heart and put a new spirit in them; I will remove from them their heart of stone and give them a heart of flesh. Then they will follow My decrees and be careful to keep My laws..."* (NIV).

We cannot walk in obedience to His decrees without first having the stones removed from our hearts and then receive more of His Spirit. This takes place when a person becomes a Christian, but I believe it is also a progressive experience in the believer's life.

As God continues to remove the heart of stone and give us His Spirit, we move ahead on the pathway to holiness. The way God removes the heart of stone is through repentance. Repenting and receiving God's forgiveness softens us—for those who are forgiven much, love much (see Luke 7:47). The ability to repent is itself rooted in love, however, and again, it is God's initiative toward us.

In love and kindness God reveals our sins; then from a heart of love, we respond by repenting. To repent means to stop from going one direction and to completely turn around and go in the opposite direction.

My friend, Pastor Bill Johnson, looks further into the origins of the word *repent*. The prefix *re* means "to do again," (such as repeat, reinvest, etc.) The word *pent* comes from a Latin word that means "penthouse" or "high place." When we *re-pent*, we are actually turning around, leaving the lower place of confusion and sin, and going back up to the high place where God meant for us to dwell.[1]

Although many may repent because of fear or feigned obedience (depending on the doctrine or environment of their Christian growth), there is no greater or more lasting repentance than that initiated through God's love. That is why Paul establishes the love of God in the first 11 chapters of Romans and then tells us in Romans 12:1: *"In view of God's mercy... offer your bodies as living sacrifices, holy and pleasing to God..."* (NIV).

True holiness and victory over sin will not take place without love as the motivating factor. For only then is our surrender complete.

Revival has brought just this kind of redemptive love into my life and the lives of countless others. God has lovingly revealed sins in my life and then poured out His Spirit in a way that has helped me overcome the very root and origin of these sins. Sins that were deeply ingrained have fallen off like shackles severed from a slave. I have never felt so free in my life.

Though the accelerated process began more than 15 years ago (when I was already 20 years old in the Lord), I felt as though I was being born again and again. People who have criticized this move of God often say, "Where is the repentance? What is the laughter all about? Why aren't you talking about sin more? Revival is not about laughter, but about repentance."

What many people do not realize is that, in this move, more true repentance has been taking place inside people's hearts than at any other time in their walk with Jesus. I know this is true in my own life.

Nothing changes us like the love of God. The goodness of God does lead to repentance (see Rom. 2:4). As Paul encouraged us, beginning in First Corinthians 12:31, love is indeed *"a more excellent way."*

Bitter Roots

It was early October 1994, the time of my first trip to Toronto. I could sense the air of excitement as thousands flew to join the Toronto Christian Fellowship for their first "Catch the Fire" Conference.

Lou Engle and I had been chomping at the bit to go to Canada since the beginning of that year. We had heard months prior about the unusual move of the Holy Spirit taking place there. Of course, we were radically touched at the Vineyard Conference in Anaheim, but we knew quickly, as did the world, that Toronto was the "new Azusa Street" for this wave of the Holy Spirit.

Indeed, thousands had already flocked to Toronto. Lou and I had been so consumed with starting a new church that we had not yet been able to visit this new "Mecca" of revival. Now we were finally on our way.

My first encounter was a bit offbeat and not quite what I had expected, at least not compared to the image of the outpouring I'd formed in my own mind. My initial experience was at a meeting held before the conference officially began. We were packed like sardines into the original fellowship building which seats 500 at most. It seemed to me that the most memorable feature of that event was my discomfort of feeling like a sardine. That was the first exposure to Toronto. But things would change dramatically in the days ahead as the conference moved to the nearby large Regal Constellation Hotel.

As Lou and I arrived in the large Constellation conference room, we were greeted by several other people from our church who had also come to Toronto. Two of them joined me in finding seats very close to the front. (I lost Lou in the crowd.) That was a miracle in itself as more than 3,000 people were present. I do not remember who spoke that night; most likely it was John Arnott. Nor do I remember what was said. I do remember, however, what happened to me during the ministry time because it changed my life forever.

When it came time for people to come forward to receive personal ministry, I almost ran up to the front. For those not familiar with the style of ministry in Toronto and in Pasadena, lines are clearly marked on the floor of the meeting place so that people can assemble in an orderly fashion, wait on the Lord, and then receive prayer from the prayer team.

My two friends and I ended up close to each other on the first row. Having been so powerfully touched by the tangible presence of God in Anaheim and knowing about the joy and manifestations spreading from Toronto, my only goal was to get blasted by the Holy Spirit. I wanted all the manifestations and more. I was so revived in January with the dose I received at the Vineyard Conference that I had to have more. I also wanted enough to bring back a fresh anointing to Harvest Rock Church.

When a member of the ministry team came up to me and started to pray, I felt a gentle presence of the Holy Spirit and soon fell down onto the carpet of the hotel meeting room. I could hear my friends laughing as they hit the floor powerfully. Frankly, I was envious. I wanted to be "drunk in the spirit,"—enjoying the "good times" as they seemed to be doing. The truth is, I felt almost nothing.

As I lay there, I asked the Lord to show me what He wanted me to receive that night. Immediately, God began to reveal bitterness in my heart toward a particular brother in the Lord. The Holy Spirit's conviction hit me so hard that I began to weep at the sinfulness of my heart. I lay there sobbing and repenting while my friends became engulfed in laughter and holy joy.

That night, God began to show me hurts I had suppressed and how, instead of confronting them, I had denied they even existed. Because the hurts were real, they developed into the "bitter roots" about which the Bible speaks in Hebrews 12:15 (NIV). Having the loving presence of the Holy Spirit ministering to me that night, I could face the pain that was too deep to acknowledge in my everyday setting and circumstances.

Though it would be difficult to walk the whole situation through to a resolution, there was now a presence, a leading, and a grace about it that I had never before experienced. In the months ahead, I was able to resolve the bitterness toward this particular brother and ask for his forgiveness for the ways in which I had wronged him. This progress in turn unearthed the foundation of an even deeper sensitivity to rejection that I'd felt from my father.

Before I tell you what happened, please let me share with you a few important things about my dad. His name is Byung Kook Ahn. My father is also a pastor, a truly great man of God. I say that not just because I am his son; those who know him recognize it also. He is a pastor who is highly respected on a national level in the Korean community both in the United States and in Korea. He was elected as the president of his church's denomination twice. He has spoken in some of the largest churches in Korea, including Full Gospel Central Church, pastored then by David Yonggi Cho. He also held a revival service at Kwang Lin Methodist church, the largest Methodist church in the world at that time (70,000 members), which was pastored by Sun Do Kim, who has also since retired.

My father has authored several books. He was also the first Korean Baptist pastor (Southern Baptist affiliate) in North America. More importantly, he is a man of character who demonstrates a love and a passion for Jesus. I can honestly say that my dad is one of the kindest, most generous, and most gracious men I know. I have tremendous respect for him and am grateful for all the sacrifices he made for his children, both as a father and as a pastor. I have a deep love for him. Today, our relationship has never been better—but it was not always that way.

In 1958, when I was only two years old, my father left my mother, four-year-old sister Chung-Hae, and me behind in Korea so he could accept a pastoral position in the Washington, D.C., area. Obviously, my father wanted his family to fly to Washington with him, but we were not granted visas. He went on ahead of us, believing for a quick resolution to a difficult separation.

It would be more than two years before we were released to join my father in the United States. During those key formative years of my life, I missed my father greatly.

I remember finally getting off the plane and eagerly running up to the man my mother pointed out to me as my dad. When he picked me up, all I could say was, "I know that you're my father, but you don't look like my father!"

It is amazing the things you remember, even after so many years. During the two years of separation from my dad, I had little opportunity to know him more; in fact, I had forgotten what he looked like.

As my childhood progressed, I do not remember spending much time with my dad. He was extremely busy pastoring and had to work a second job as a dental technician to support his family. Working two full-time jobs, pastoring a church, and taking care of a family in a new country, placed my father under enormous stress.

My father's motives for coming to the United States were to leave a war-torn country and to provide a good education and future for his family. My sister Chung-Hae was an excellent student. I was a slow learner, though, and struggled in school. When I brought home mediocre report cards, I was physically punished by my father for not trying harder. It was not long before I resented my father. I felt rejected by him. The rejection led to my looking for acceptance elsewhere; I found it among my friends at school. I was always popular, and I was always a leader (as far as I can remember). I guess God had given me those leadership qualities from birth. However, I soon led my friends into lawlessness and rebellion. Drugs, sex, and rock and roll became my pagan lifestyle.

I do not blame my father for being upset about my rebellious ways. I *was* rebellious. Unfortunately, my rebellion only led to more physical punishment and more feelings of rejection and resentment. When I came to Christ, I tried to work through much of the pain from those turbulent pre-conversion years. I remember going to a Bill Gothard "Basic Institute in Youth Conflicts" Ministry Conference. I came home and asked my father and my mother to forgive me for all the pain I had caused them. They gladly forgave me, but I never confronted my father for the pain he had caused me.

While on the floor in Toronto, God began to reveal an entire arena of bitterness in my heart connected to the hurts I still carried from my father. I realized I needed to talk to my father, but I did not have the courage to initiate the conversation. Finally, the right opportunity came when my father and mother flew to Pasadena for my brother Chae-Woo's wedding in November of 1996.

Little did I know that I was about to experience firsthand the fulfillment of the following prophesy from Malachi:

> *See, I will send you the prophet Elijah before that great and dreadful day of the Lord comes. He will turn the hearts of the fathers to*

their children, and the hearts of the children to their fathers; or else
I will come and strike the land with a curse (Malachi 4:5-6 NIV).

Malachi prophesied that God would release the spirit of Elijah on His people. This word came with a prophetic invitation for us to turn our hearts to our children in reconciliation and likewise turn our hearts to our fathers so that we would experience revival. If we do not accept this invitation, the land will be cursed with judgment.

My Malachi 4:6 Experience

I was very nervous throughout the day I had planned to talk with my father. I was not sure how I could communicate to him the hurts I had carried for 24 years. Just asking him to meet with me took all the nerve I could muster. Realizing how difficult it was to communicate with him showed me how deep and serious the hurts were in my life.

"Dad, can I talk with you privately?" I asked.

"Sure, son. Why don't you drive me to the hotel and we can talk on the way?" he replied.

I could not get into the conversation as we drove to the Pasadena Hilton. I wanted to talk to him face-to-face, not while I was driving. Finally, as I pulled the car into the hotel parking lot, I turned off the engine, and I began to pour out my heart to him.

"Dad, I need to communicate something that is very difficult to express. Please know that before I begin, I want to say I deeply love and honor you." I took a deep breath and I began. "Dad, I am still hurting over the rejection I felt when you physically punished me as I was growing up. I feel that you crossed the line, and as a pastor today, I realize that you physically abused me."

There was immediate sadness in my father's eyes. I could almost see his tears welling up. "After all these years, you are still hurt over what happened when you were a kid?" he inquired incredulously.

"Yes, Dad," I continued. "Dad, you don't have to respond to what I am sharing with you. Just getting this off my chest and expressing something I have wanted to say for a long time is healing enough," I concluded.

My father and I talked for several more minutes. He shared with me how those years of striving to survive as immigrants in America were very stressful years for him. He revealed to me that he had also been abused by his mother, who had a violent temper. Interestingly enough, his father had never hit him. I confessed that I had not been a model kid, and we both had a good laugh about that understatement. We hugged each other, expressed our appreciation for one another, and then he went into the hotel.

I drove home elated, but more good news was yet to come. A few minutes after I arrived home, my mother called me from the hotel. She was crying on the phone— for me.

"Ché, I am so sorry that you are still feeling pain over something that happened so long ago," she began.

"Mom, I am OK now. I just had to share my heart with Dad. Just talking to him has made me feel so much better," I replied.

Then she asked my forgiveness for not protecting me from my father's anger. "I wanted to protect you and stop your father from hitting you, but as a pastor's wife and an Asian woman, I could not interfere."

I told her, "Mom there is nothing to forgive. I totally understand the difficult situation you were in."

Then she told me that my father wanted to talk to me. She handed him the phone. I was surprised by that. Immediately, fear came into my heart. My first thought was that Dad was mad at me for exposing him.

Instead, what happened next is something I will never forget for the rest of my life. As my father picked up the phone, he said with deep compassion words I had never heard him say and ever expected to hear him say. "Son, what I did to you as you were growing up was wrong. Will you ever forgive me?" he queried.

I was stunned. I could hardly believe what I was hearing. I regained my composure enough to respond and assure him that, of course, I forgave him. Then he added, "Son, you know how proud I am of you. And I love you very much."

I was so shocked by what I was hearing that I didn't know whether to cry, laugh, or shout.

"Dad, I love you, too," was my only reply. It was the first time I had ever heard the words *I love you* from my father. We said goodbye, and as soon as I hung up the phone—I kid you not—I pumped my arm and shouted "Yes!" and then proceeded to dance around the room.

No words can describe the effect this encounter has had on my life. A spirit of rejection was broken off me forever. To this very day, I am seeing and feeling the fruit of this reconciliation. The Scriptures say that God will turn the hearts of the fathers to the children and the hearts of the children to the fathers before Christ comes back (see Mal. 4:6). That is exactly what I have experienced and what many others are experiencing during this current move of the Spirit. I believe this is surely a sign of the end-time revival.

When I see such life-altering events as this being experienced by so many believers, I can't help but be perturbed by criticism that points to this revival as a laughing revival. Yes, God is pouring out His joy; after all, the Kingdom of God is *"righteousness and peace and joy in the Holy Spirit"* (Rom. 14:17).

My experience and observation tell me that He is also doing a deep work of convicting us of our sin so that we can resolve previously unaddressed root issues that will defile many if left to grow (see Heb. 12:15; 1 John 1:10). This conviction is bringing tremendous freedom and sanctification to many.

Though this newfound liberty and reconciliation with my father were indescribably wonderful, this was only the beginning of a progressively profound change in my personal life that would especially alter my relationship with my wife, Sue, and others. I believe that our relationships with our fathers affect every relationship in our lives—especially our relationship with God and with those closest to us. That is why addressing the paternal relationship first can bring so much wonderful transformation.

Regarding my relationship with Sue, God healed our marriage in deep areas I didn't even know were broken. (So broken, in fact, that Sue had closed her heart to me and I couldn't even understand why!) Sue forgave me for my behavior, religious attitudes, and hurtful actions. (I also forgave her for the ways in which she had hurt me.) It took work and counseling, but it was a great investment. (I have an awesome marriage to prove it!) Today, we continue to live a vulnerable and honest life before one another and before others with whom we share accountability.

My prayer for you is that you, too, will be reconciled to your family members, especially where your father and (if you are a father) where your children are concerned. At the end of the day, what really matters in life are relationships. Your relationships with God and your family members are precious gifts that can make all the difference in your life—for better or for worse.

Even if your family is not ready to talk things out like I did with my father and with Sue, you can begin by asking God for the grace to repent of all bitterness and judgment. Ask for a fresh revelation of the Father heart of God.

God is our loving heavenly Father. I don't believe that we can truly love without really receiving the revelation of how much the Father loves us. The Bible says, *"We love because He first loved us"* (1 John 4:19 NIV). That is why I intentionally and regularly hold conferences on the Father Heart of God. We also have extensive inner healing ministries to help people come into wholeness. We are not the "only game in town," so check out what may be available in your area.

Of course, you are welcome to attend one of our conferences. You can find more information about the resources that are available through our church ministry by visiting our website at harvestrockchurch.org.

I pray that you, too, will walk this path of love, acceptance, and forgiveness. Doing so will unlock your true significance, godly love, and power!

Endnote

1. Bill Johnson, *The Supernatural Power of a Transformed Mind* (Shippensburg, PA: Destiny Image, 2005), 44.

CHAPTER 9

Hooray for Hollywood!

Everyone in Pasadena had driven past the place, including me.

You could see it in television shots from the Rose Parade. Indeed, it was the "Crown Jewel" of Pasadena—the beautiful Ambassador Auditorium on the former campus of the Worldwide Church of God.

The fountain which adorned the expansive lawns of the property could take your breath away as its waters cascaded downward. The white marble pillars all around the glass and marble building drew passersby to want to look inside.

The building had been empty for seven years, ever since the reformation of the Worldwide Church of God. Builders had fought over the property for years, making huge bids for it, but to no avail. Multimillion-dollar condos had been planned in many an entrepreneur's mind; all of them had their hopes dashed. Corporations pictured themselves centered on the beautiful campus with the jealous eyes of less fortunate businesses watching them. They too, were unsuccessful at acquiring the property.

In the midst of an overcrowded Southern California, here stood one last bastion of God's prime real estate—and the WCG had already decided that the property would not be used for anything other than God's purposes.

Little did I know that their plans for the building would include us. However, the timing was fitting; we were growing unsettled in our meeting place. Mott Auditorium, a brick, fortress-like structure from the 1940s, had served us well. Still, it was getting to be time to move on.

Mott had the largest seating capacity in the city. It was functional, but by no means pretty. Still, we were grateful for it! We had seen hundreds of nights of revival services and welcomed thousands of believers and unbelievers alike from all over the world during a variety of conferences, outreaches, and regular services during the ten years we had rented the facility.

The spacious floor near the front podium had ample room for those who wanted to "soak" in the Spirit. People were able to lie on the floor in God's presence and "drink Him in" like thirsty camels who'd come a long way for refreshment. We even had a special carpet with colored lines to mark where those awaiting prayer should stand. The colors were carefully arranged so that, when people fell in the Spirit, they wouldn't fall on anyone else! With special markings spaced seven feet apart to ensure safety, it was America's first "renewal carpet!"

In fact, the first Fire Tunnel took place at Mott Auditorium. John Arnott was the speaker, and we had more than 2,000 people in attendance. To say the least, the leadership team was tired. We had promised to personally minister to everyone there. We needed God's help and fast! I had this idea that we would just have people form a line while the leaders would line up facing each other to create a "tunnel" for them to walk through. The leaders would lay hands on each person, praying or prophesying as the line of people kept moving. Many never made it though the line on their feet. They would get hit with the power of God the moment they entered the Fire Tunnel. We soon had to employ volunteer "bouncers" to pull people through and keep the line moving!

John thought this was such a good idea that he exported it to Toronto. The Fire Tunnel concept then spread throughout the world. John would often state that his first Fire Tunnel experience was at Mott. I often have stated that our contribution to this revival was birthing the Fire Tunnel. It works especially well when anointed children man it!

We had wonderful memories from our years at Mott. Children had seen angelic visitations around the tall ceiling beams for more than six months. The flags of all the nations hung proudly around the entire arena. Since the building had no air conditioning, we would often leave the doors open during services. Gentle singing could be heard as far as a block away. Often, after hearing the inviting music, ethnic neighbors would simply come in and join us. The casual atmosphere and open doors were welcoming.

Yet renting the facility was becoming increasingly difficult. First of all, the price was steep; at that time the rent was $35,000 a month. Also, I firmly believe in possessing property rather than renting it, if at all possible. It makes for a better investment. We had also outgrown the parking facilities or lack thereof. There were no official parking lots. Instead, cars could be found strewn in every direction within blocks of the church. Many people gave up or didn't come to events because parking was so difficult. One speaker even quipped "You'd have to have a search warrant to find the place." It was clear that we were outgrowing our secret nest. We knew God had other plans.

Harvest Rock Church had always had a particular penchant to see Hollywood transformed. We had special home groups with that emphasis; these groups were attended both by those who worked in the industry and by those interested in its conversion.

Always, there were films being made in the area where Mott stood. We were frequently reminded that, for better or worse, Hollywood greatly affects the world. In addition, countless prophetic ministers had addressed me and different members of our church about God's plan for us to reach Tinsel Town.

I had never equated any of those factors with the issue of any building we might own. Yet God had, and the Ambassador Auditorium was privately offered to us at an incredible price—not to rent, but to own.

I knew then and I know now that God usually calls us to do things we believe are way over our heads. As far as I was concerned, the idea of buying the Ambassador Auditorium was not only over my head, it wasn't even in this stratosphere.

While out of town with my wife, I received an urgent call from the President of Maranatha High School, a Christian institution with whom we had shared the campus of Mott Auditorium. They, too, were looking for a new facility. He suggested that we incorporate together and purchase the whole Ambassador campus! Together, we could work on an offer that neither of us might have ventured to execute individually.

For this deal to work, we would have to have a substantial down payment by January 1, with the balance due in May. It was a limited-time offer. I had no time to call our pastors; I had to make an executive decision. I quickly prayed with my wife Sue and made an "apostolic" decision. I told our prospective partner, "I am in!"

Things progressed quickly, and we went to see the facilities. The auditorium had been maintained like a King's palace, even though it had been vacant for some time. As we entered the structure, we were struck with the magnificence of the huge, one-of-a-kind chandelier. We walked on handmade wool carpet from India; viewed the greatest array of pink onyx in one building in the Western hemisphere; spotted exquisite teak panels from Africa; and stood in awe of the 24-carat gold overlay that adorned the ceilings and sound baffles.

The building has been compared to the Kennedy Center and the Dorothy Chandler Pavilion for its beauty and elaborate finish alone. As a Pasadena landmark, it has hosted such arts events as concerts by Luciano Pavarotti, Arthur Rubenstein, Pearl Bailey, Mel Torme, Bing Crosby, and The Vienna Orchestra.

Did God have a purpose in opening this facility to us? I quickly began to see in prayer that this building could provide a strong connection for us with our community and with Hollywood.

For virtually less than half its value, we would be able to buy the building and continue to share it with the greater Los Angeles area. God planted some amazing ideas in my mind: Why not continue to make this facility available for public events? Why not rent it out to artists and organizations while adding God into the rental equation?

The thought that came to mind was to have a rental arrangement for special events in which the contract specified that I or one of our staff members would be permitted to hold daily devotions and share the Gospel with our rental guests. That way, we would not only be able to pay our bank note, we would also have additional opportunities to share the Gospel!

It sounded like a great idea, but where were the funds going to come from? What happened next was something even I had trouble believing. In order to possess the building, I needed to produce, in four months' time, a $4.5 million cash down payment. We had already put down a $1 million security deposit. If we didn't come up with the remaining $3.5 million, we would lose the security deposit. I have to admit, I had fleeting visions of being run out of town for losing a million dollars in a risky venture. These worrisome images flashed across my mind more than once.

Still, I had a peace that God was in this challenge with us. Even in the midst of raising the millions, there was a supernatural grace and an assurance that He would both provide and receive the glory. Even down to the wire, with just four days to go, we still had $1.3 million left to raise. The pastors asked how we were going to pull it off. Before I could "retrieve" the words from my mouth, they came out: "It's a done deal."

My heart had made its statement of faith; and in the end, God parted our "Red Sea." Through the generosity of dear friends, the money came through. By 4 P.M. on May 14th, we had all of it. We quickly wired the funds and consummated the purchase of our magnificent property. May 14, 2004 was the day Harvest Rock Church became the proud owners of one of the world's premiere performance arts buildings!

This began the fulfillment of our dream to reach Hollywood. One of our first major leases was from the cast and crew of *Dream Girls,* the Hollywood movie about the life of singer Diana Ross. Beyonce played the lead role. I'll never forget when my wife, Sue, and I prayed with her personally and shared with her what God had put in our hearts during our devotional!

We have also had NBC and MTV rent the auditorium. We've had major ensembles, such as the L.A. Chamber Orchestra, perform at Ambassador. We've had Governor Schwarzenegger and sports stars like Derek Fisher of the L.A. Lakers speak at our auditorium.

And each time, I stand up and introduce the event by sharing the Gospel!

People who would never come to a church building have come to ours. By contract, we are to share the Gospel—and to date, not a single organization has refused this contractual condition!

We also meet every Sunday at the Ambassador and hold all types of other weekly church meetings there. We have drawn media attention because of the beautiful facility; I believe it "lends" our charismatic services and our gracious God a sense of increased credibility in the eyes of those in the surrounding city, throughout Hollywood, and even the world!

People have said that purchasing Ambassador Auditorium is a prophetic sign of the beginning of the great transfer of wealth prophesied in passages such as Isaiah 60:5,11; Proverbs 13:22; and Haggai 2:7. It is also a sign that God wants us to bring reformation to the mountain of Media and the mountain of Arts and Entertainment. The hosting of famous orchestras and artists by Harvest Rock Church provides a way for us to do our small part in bringing about the transformation and reformation of society.

In a later chapter of this book, I'll share how this facet of ministry fits the bigger vision of our destiny. Our acquisition of the Ambassador Auditorium is an example of how God causes us to be effective. We've learned not to be afraid of visible significance when God is the One who opens the door.

That's good advice for all of us!

CHAPTER 10

Answering "TheCall"

The Lord awoke me five hours into the night with a startling question: "Are you willing to drop everything and help your brother Lou?"

God was referring to Lou Engle, my associate pastor and covenant brother with whom I'd been joined in ministry since 1983. Lou was obeying God and walking straight into the convergence of his destiny: the assignment to bring TheCall to our nation and, in time, the world.

Shortly after the renowned Promise Keeper's "Stand in the Gap" event held in Washington, D.C., in 1997, Lou received a prophetic vision from the Lord. It was a vision of a youth counterpart to events like "Stand in the Gap." In the vision, Lou saw a gathering of countless faces at the National Mall in Washington, D.C.

Lou had always envisioned stadiums filled to capacity with young people gathering for solemn assemblies during which they would pray and fast for revival. This was, of course, Lou's passion and lifestyle and a burden he was willing to bear.

I will never forget what happened when we first moved to the Los Angeles area to start a church; that was when Lou first joined in ministry with me, my wife Sue, and a few others. Lou didn't quite fit the mold as a pastor, evangelist, or administrator. He wasn't the "multi-hat" type of person you pray for when you start a church planting team on a limited budget.

But he was exactly what we needed. The Lord showed me that this prophet was a consecrated man whose life was to be given to prayer and fasting. In a nutshell, that is Lou's story. Much like the prophets of old, his voice is God's clarion call to righteousness and justice for everyone alive in this generation.

This became more apparent as God began to fuel Lou's dreams. After he saw the vision for a gathering on the National Mall, Lou began preaching it. Soon he was imparting the dream in youth conferences across the nation. In Phoenix, Arizona, the spirit of prayer fell so profoundly upon the young people that they began to cry out for the fulfillment of the dream.

In the spring of 1999, a woman who had never heard Lou preach approached him and inquired, "Have you ever considered organizing a massive gathering of youth in Washington, D.C., to pray for America?"

Stunned, and without hesitation, Lou exclaimed, "Lady, I've been preaching that vision all across America."

"Fantastic," the woman replied, "because I would like to give you $100,000 as seed money to get the vision started." Right there, on that unforgettable spot, the woman scribbled out a check for $50,000 and mailed Lou the balance shortly thereafter.

I remember Lou's face as clearly as if it were yesterday; he showed me the check, explained what had happened, and said, "What do I do now, Ché?"

Being the consummate detail man, I simply said, "Establish an organizational name. Open a bank account. Deposit the money. Find a national youth leader to organize the gathering in Washington, D.C. Go for it."

It sounded simple enough to me, but you have to know Lou. Someone once commented that Lou is like one of the sky-born characters in the Macy's day parade. In a very good and needed way, he is in the high places with God most of the time; but he needs between 40 and 70 handlers on the ground to keep him on track.

Knowing this, I kindly but firmly told Lou, "You know I'll support you in prayer. I'll even ask Harvest Rock Church to help fund the project. But with all that is on my plate as senior pastor, with HIM internationally, and with conferences and other ministry obligations, there is no way I can be involved, except in an advisory role."

You've heard the old axiom, "Never say 'never' to God," right? I'm sure by now you know the rest of the story. By mid-fall that year, Lou still had not found an apostle to organize TheCall. I could see the burden was taking a toll on him. Not only was he losing sleep, he was dropping more weight than he could afford to lose.

God woke me up that memorable night and reminded me that I had once again consecrated everything to Him—just the night before in a service I preached. I was hoping to get off the hook of "dropping everything to help Lou" by advising God that my wife and children would have to be in agreement with the idea. (Surely, they'd say, "No." They had too much on their plates, too!)

I saw flashes of myself traveling for weeks at a time, away from my family and church, raising millions of dollars for a project that I didn't initiate, and not being sure I could do it, to boot.

The Lord knew better. One of my children said, "Dad, Uncle Lou has served you all these years; of course you should help him." With the confirmation of my family, I met with the pastors of Harvest Rock. With their blessings, I said "Yes" to Lou. He and his wife Therese wept with tears of joy at the news that we were on board.

Write the Vision

With support from my family, the pastors, staff, and members of Harvest Rock Church, Lou and I began to mobilize. Our first step was to seek God and write a vision statement: "TheCall is a solemn assembly bringing together two generations for the purpose of praying and fasting for revival and transformation of our cities and our nation."[1]

Thus began the historic journey of TheCall, a ministry that has become known around the world. TheCall encompasses many countries, many cultures, and many generations. Each Call event has had a different flavor and emphasis; there have been notable testimonies of transformation, and cultural shifts have been noted after each event.

The vision of TheCall has expanded to include the shaping of history through prayer and fasting (see Joel 2), the turning of the hearts of fathers to the children and the hearts of children to the fathers (see Mal. 4:5-6), and the raising up of the next generation to be leaders in every sector of society (the seven mountains: education, government, media, the economy, religion, arts and entertainment, and family).

These areas have been given over to a secular, godless reign. Believers, hindered by a lack of knowledge, have abdicated their authority and influence over society. God is calling all of us to rise as leaders in our respective fields so that His righteous rule can again become our nation's foundation.

TheCall is doing an awesome job of helping to birth radical transformers who are full of the Spirit and His power...and are willing to pay the price.

Hearing TheCall

The first Call, known as "TheCall D.C.," was the greatest ministry challenge I had ever encountered. It was also my most rewarding ministry experience.

We had chosen to shoot for a September event just months away because of the seriousness of the upcoming elections at that time. Many people advised us to wait a year so we'd have more time to put the event together; yet the promptings of God are not always so seemingly logical. Our hope was to challenge young people to maintain 40 days of fasting and prayer for our nation; these 40 days would lead right up to Election Day.

Afterward, when the presidential election made history due to its bizarre vote count and the delayed electoral victory for President Bush, I felt assured that the prayer and fasting of those youths had made a true difference in the electoral outcome. As I will share later in this chapter, I believe many of the Calls have produced similarly significant and almost immediate results.

Only God could have mobilized the volunteer teams and the 400,000 youth and adults who were estimated to be in attendance at that first Call. We knew it was the Holy Spirit alone. We could only say, *"This is the Lord's doing; it is marvelous in our eyes"* (Ps.118:23 KJV).

Hand to the Plow

While putting together an event intended to draw tens or hundreds of thousands to an open-air venue for just one day may seem simple, it is anything but. God hand-selected an awesome Executive Board to complete the main work of organizing the first Call. He also chose countless volunteers who served in every area of responsibility. God has stepped in to do the same for every subsequent event.

Think about all it entails: you need a prayer team; volunteers and their coordinators; a media team; a mobilization team that will bring the participants together; a facilities and events team to handle logistics; all the necessary marketing to get the word out; a website crew; musicians, speakers, and sound crew; parking attendants; water "warriors"; and so much more—including the much-needed porta-potty people!

My heart desires to name each and every person who gave their time, effort, and finances to answer God's call at each event and who came to fast and pray and make history. Yet, lack of space prohibits. I can truly say that each and every name is recorded in God's book, and like many of those we find in the Bible, they will be remembered forever. My thanks again to you personally if you are among those who have put their hand to this work of God's heart.

The Day That Changed America: 9/2/2000

When the day of "TheCall D.C." arrived, none of us knew what to expect. We only knew that God had told us to gather a holy convocation, and we had done everything the Spirit directed to get the word out. We truly had no idea whether 50 people or 50,000 people would show up. When you are inviting the youth, it usually takes a concert or something spectacular to get them up before dawn to spend a day in the hot sun.

Add to that the fact that we made a special point of *not* featuring any of the musicians who would lead worship (though we had awesome "names" who gladly gave their time). We billed the gathering honestly, calling it a "fast, not a feast," and we asked for dawn-to-dusk prayer. All things considered, we knew only God could amass a group of people who were *that* hungry for change.

When I reached the stage on the Mall at 5:30 A.M., it was still dark. Yet it was apparent that the D.C. Mall was already packed with people. The logistics coordinator of TheCall rushed over with exhilarating news: "Ché, I estimate there are already 270,000 people here. The report is that the subway is jammed with more and people are still arriving." A chill went up my spine!

At 6 A.M. sharp, the gathering began with my son Gabriel leading our youth band in worship. God's glory was thick enough to cut with a knife.

At this event, there was a grace to call us into prayer and repentance unequal to any other I have ever experienced. For 12 hours we worshiped, repented, prayed, and were challenged by some of the top speakers in our nation—all of whom came at their own expense. While the tone was serious (we recognized the state of our country and of our own hearts), there was an inexplicable hope and awe that God could turn around any situation with this kind of unity, worship, and prayer.

The stage hosted every kind of person that day. Hispanics, African-Americans, Asians, Caucasians, young, old. Different types of worship and many different styles of prayer went forth. We were joined by many well-known Christians; but most of those in attendance were "nameless" and "faceless."

Some lay on stage on their faces, pleading with God; others reverently stood on their feet respectfully imploring Him; multiplied thousands sat or stood side by side in the hot sun for hours conjoined by the presence of the Spirit without measure. No one who attended will ever forget it; and the vision birthed that day continues to grow in each heart.

Something shifted on that day of TheCall D.C. That historic first Call was followed by a contested and historic election. It yielded the Supreme Court decision that proclaimed George W. Bush the winner of the presidential election. A further implication of the election outcome is the fact that President Bush selected two Supreme Court Justices—Chief Justice Roberts and Associate Justice Alito. These men tipped the balance to ban partial-birth abortion.

Truly, you could see before your eyes the fulfillment of Second Chronicles 7:14:

> *If My people who are called by My name will humble themselves, and pray and seek My face, and turn from their wicked ways, then I will hear from heaven and will forgive their sin and will heal their land.*

As Walter Wink, professor emeritus at Auburn Theological Seminary in New York, said, "History belongs to the intercessors."[2] I believe we made history that day.

TheCall Continues

Instilled with new fire in my heart, I must confess I breathed a great sigh of relief when this monumental event was over. I was also grateful for what God had accomplished through TheCall toward His Kingdom purposes for our nation.

Surely God would have said "Well done, good and faithful servant. Enter into your rest" (see Matt. 25:23). After all, He knew better than anyone the 24/7 schedule I seemed to keep. He'd heard about it enough through my continual "prayers."

Yet I soon found out that what I thought was an ending was actually just the beginning. Along came Lou with a sheepish-looking grin announcing, "Ché, I believe we're supposed to have other Call events to confront the false ideologies of our society. I feel certain the next one should be in New England to confront the liberalism in the Ivy League universities. I mean, Ché, most of these schools began with a Christian foundation. Let's take back for God what the enemy has stolen. We can do that through fasting and prayer."

Knowing Lou, I wasn't surprised to hear the request. Knowing God, I wasn't surprised to know I would be involved in the answer. What began as a reluctant but obedient "yes" to help my friend evolved into three years of serious work to help change a nation and the generations. With a workable style intact, Lou continues to have Call events, as do teams in other nations. I attend and participate as I am able, although I no longer need to be involved in hands-on orchestration and administration.

I am convinced these vital, ongoing summonses from God are a crucial answer to the devastating problems facing us all. We have had many Calls since September 2, 2000; apart from the first Call, the one in San Diego was the most significant for me.

TheCall San Diego took place on November 1, 2008, in Qualcomm Stadium. Again, we were facing an important election, but for me the real issue was to pass Proposition 8 in California. This resolution defines marriage exclusively as a union between one man and one woman, making same-sex marriage illegal. This proposition has huge ramifications for the United States. California is often at the forefront of change, leading the rest of the nation. In fact, it has been said, "As California goes, so goes the United States."

We knew we had to pass Prop 8. Many believers didn't understand that if the measure lost, then the freedom of speech of pastors to speak out on the issue of homosexuality would have been taken away; their preaching and teaching against homosexuality would have been classified as "hate speech." Not only that, but teachers in elementary schools would have felt themselves to be under legal obligation to teach same-sex marriage as an alternative lifestyle. We knew much was at stake.

I would be naive to think only prayer and fasting would pass Prop 8. Millions of dollars needed to be raised to counter the media blitz staged by the opposition. I thank God for Ron Prentice and ProtectMarriage.com who diligently succeeded in that project, and for Pastor Jim Garlow of Skyline Wesleyan Church who mobilized thousands of pastors and 100,000 volunteers in support of the proposition. It took a massive united effort to fight for God's definition of marriage!

Yet I believe the final shift to pass Prop 8 took place at TheCall San Diego, which took place only three days before the vote. At that point, pollsters called the issue a dead heat.

Around 4:15 P.M. on the day of TheCall San Diego, I felt that something significant had shifted in the spiritual atmosphere after praying and fasting all day. I turned to Lou and said, "I believe we are going to win Prop 8. I just know it in my spirit." Dutch Sheets and Jim Garlow agreed that the battle was won that day at TheCall.

Proposition 8 was passed by a significant margin on November 4; the final tally was 52 percent to 48 percent. This strong outcome occurred even though Prop 8 had been running 10 percent behind in the polls just a month earlier. Truly, history belongs to the intercessors!

From East to West

Just as TheCall San Diego impacted history, so have the others which have taken place at key times and key locations. While it is not possible to include a comprehensive summary, here is an overview of several significant Calls held in our nation.

TheCall New England focused on re-digging the wells of the Great Awakening while closing the doors to false ideologies, religious heresies, and the intellectual pride that came through the gates of higher learning. (Many Ivy League universities were originally founded to send missionaries out and bring in Christian ideologies.)

TheCall New York called for repentance for removing prayer from our schools via the 1962 landmark Supreme Court case, a case that originated in New York. This Call also sought to re-dig the wells of revival and noontime prayer meetings begun by Jeremiah Lamphier in the mid-1850s. That revival saw millions come to the Lord in the United States and United Kingdom. There was also prayer for righteousness to be established on Wall Street and for repentance of selfishness and covetous materialism!

TheCall Kansas City focused on returning the heart of America to bridal love and intimacy with Jesus, while TheCall Los Angeles sought to re-dig the wells of the awesome movements that changed the world. These historic movements all began in California: the Azusa Street Revival of 1906; the Jesus Movement that began in the late 1960s; the ministry of Aimee Semple McPherson and the Foursquare Church; the influence of Calvary Chapel, the Vineyard, and others. We also prayed for repentance of the Christian abdication of authority in the media and for forgiveness for sexual immorality and pornography. (Los Angeles is the world capital for disseminating these abominations.)

Next came TheCall San Francisco, which began on the tail of a 40-day fast. The focus was repentance for greed and the literal "gold digging" which began in the area two centuries ago and is fostered today by the hi-tech industry. We ardently prayed for mercy against repeat judgment on the city which had already been destroyed by the fires and earthquakes of 1906.

TheCall Dallas was the site used to repent for The Sand Creek Massacre (also known as the Chivington Massacre, the Battle of Sand Creek, or the Massacre of Cheyenne Indians). On November 29, 1864, during the U.S. Indian Wars, Colorado Territory militia attacked and destroyed a village of Cheyenne and Arapaho encamped in southeastern Colorado Territory. Based on the oral history of Southern Cheyenne Chief Laird Cometsevah, around 400 Cheyenne and Arapaho men, women, and children were killed at Sand Creek. More than 700 American soldiers were involved.

One hundred and thirty-nine years after the massacre, Senator Sam Brownback represented the Senate in a first-time ever bowing in repentance before a Native American Chief, Chief Jay Swallow, a descendant of a massacred tribe that had been given documents by President Lincoln to be peace keepers before their destruction. We believe that the killing of Native Americans and the forced relocation of native peoples to government-designated reservations (including those relocations considered to be part of The Trail of Tears) opened the doors in this nation for civil rights injustice, murder, and even abortion. Intense prayer was also offered to repent for the 1973 Supreme Court Decision in the case of *Roe v. Wade*, a case originating with a lawsuit brought in Dallas in 1970.

TheCall Nashville literally gathered 70,000 on 7/7/07 to repent for ungodly music and the rebellious lifestyle that began in the 1960s with the changes produced by rock and roll. Intergenerational repentance was powerful as fathers and sons and mothers and daughters asked forgiveness for lifestyles that have destroyed much of the spirit and godliness of our youth—including drugs and abortion. Much prayer was offered for reconciliation among generations, races, religions, and more. We also called for Nashville to be known, not just for music, but for worship. Three hundred shofars blown in unity at the close of the gathering ushered in a new sound of God for America.

Significant Results

After these Calls, many significant results ensued that seem directly related to the prayer and fasting.

Consider the historic contested election that declared George Bush the winner of the 2000 presidential election. Also, consider the further implications—his appointment of two pro-life Supreme Court justices who tipped the balance in favor of banning partial birth abortion.

Consider the Wall Street dilemma; could it be that in the fullness of time, God has begun to shake out the god of mammon in this nation and establish His own rule instead?

How about San Francisco? California was in desperate straits, financially and governmentally. Prayer was offered that God would either save Governor Davis or remove him. The *next day,* a recall petition began and within six months we had a new governor.

And, of course, I thank God for passing Proposition 8, which defines marriage in agreement with the Word of God.

International Calls

In addition to the gatherings held in our nation, there have also been awesome Calls in Korea, the Philippines, Germany, Australia, Israel, and England. More are scheduled worldwide.

Transformation and Reformation

Perhaps the greatest ongoing effect of TheCalls is that they forever change those who get involved. The world desperately needs change; nothing promotes change like confronting the idols in your own heart first.

Those who participate in TheCall find that they wind up doing just that. We believe TheCall has envisioned and released those who are willing to consecrate their lives to become a "hinge of history." We have seen a whole new breed of believer that is personally consecrated and entirely in love with Jesus. This radical love impacts others. Hearts are won when believers are more interested in attending an all-day fast in the hot sun than in attending a rally at the mall with friends or spending time playing video games.

I believe the Lord has chosen TheCall in this hour to sound clarion mandates and fasts that are not only raising up this generation's Luthers, Wesleys, and Finneys, but are perhaps giving us a reprieve, sending us a blessing instead of a terrible curse (see Joel 2:14 NLT).

I am truly grateful to everyone who takes part in these Calls and who continues to live the standards of what God is calling forth through them. In an hour when more than 60 million lives have been casually extinguished through abortion, when honor and respect are lost between generations, and murder is a rite of passage in gangs, we must thank God for those who are willing to stand in the gap and say "No more!"

At a time when divorce is almost the standard, premarital sex is viewed as sport, greed is rampant, drug abuse is entertainment, and *sin* is a meaningless word, let's thank God for those who are willing to live by the Spirit that is opposite to the spirit of the world. In an age when idolatry blinds people to the face of God, pornography snares the hearts of men, and injustice still reigns in prideful hearts, what a blessing it is to find those who are captured by God alone.

It is our hope that these Calls not only change hearts and lives, but also bring permanent transformation and reformation to the root sickness of cultures while fostering reconciliation between genders, generations, denominations, and races.

The nations belong to God; it is our privilege to help the nations return to Him. For then we have truly given ourselves to His purposes in this hour. Have you?

My association with TheCall remains today one of the greatest honors and privileges in my years of serving the Lord. Thank you Lou and Therese Engle for your sacrifice of prayer and fasting to shape our nation and the world.

(For more information and for the history of TheCall, visit the ministry's website at thecall.com)

Endnotes

1. Ché Ahn and Lou Engle, *The Call Revolution* (Colorado Springs, CO: Wagner Publication, 2001), 17.

2. Walter Wink, "History Belongs to the Intercessors," *Sojourners*, October 1990.

CHAPTER 11

Media Mania

The thought of living in a media age that could fuel a new kind of Christian reformation would have exceeded my wildest dreams as a young believer.

Our world is experiencing a revolution in technology. People go about their business with small earphones and tucked away cell phones invisibly accessed as they seemingly talk into the empty air.

Computers that once were the size of a home office are now the size of small books—with all the capacity (and more) of the old models. Gone are the days of the television antenna; we have entered the world of high definition and powerful cable—accessible via handheld devices. These too will become dinosaurs in a matter of years as newer devices take their place.

Many people falsely believe that the airwaves belong to the dark ruler of this world. The Scripture calls satan *"the prince of the power of the air"* (Eph. 2:2). By no means do I interpret this verse to ascribe ownership of the airwaves to Beelzebub. I see it as more of an incentive to take back any influence satan has appropriated in this arena and to see every media method used for the Kingdom of our Christ. Media can first bring transformation to the individual, both in salvation and personal growth. Then, as the quantity and efficacy of righteous programming increases, media can bring reformation to every area of society.

Consider how media has changed the world since the invention of the printing press by Johannes Gutenberg in 1436. Gutenberg's machine forever changed the way information would be accessed. For the first time in history, people everywhere could obtain printed materials. Theoretically, everyone could have a Bible. The *Gutenberg Bible* was the first book published by Gutenberg! To this day, year in and year out, the Bible remains the most widely published book *in the earth*.

The printing press not only changed the spread of Christianity, but advanced the progress of many other "mountains" of society. As Mary Bellis notes in her writings on Inventors at About.com:

> This method of printing can be credited not only for a revolution in the production of books, but also for fostering rapid development in the sciences, arts and religion through the transmission of texts.[1]

Right now, we are in the midst of another incredible media revolution. This one is even more shocking! It is the transmission of the Gospel—*with current revival*—through television, satellite, cable, and most recently, through live programs and video streaming on the *internet!*

The effects can be seen in just one God invasion—the live internet transmission of the Lakeland Revival. God TV, whose network airs in more than 200 countries, estimated a staggering 800 percent growth in online viewers from 25,000 weekly hits to 200,000!

Millions watched the Lakeland Revival on a given night. Although controversial, the Lakeland Revival reached more people around the world during their short duration than any revival in history—because of the power of media.

Stephen Strader, pastor of the Lakeland Revival host church, says the following in his book *The Lakeland Outpouring:*

God TV continued to broadcast the night services, with about 50,000 more people watching online. The amazing thing is that *those* 50,000 a day were merely on the website. There were *millions* more watching on God TV![2]

In just a matter of weeks, people who had never heard or seen revival were huddled around their computers watching the power of God bring healing to the blind, strength to the lame, and a total touch of the Holy Spirit to the hungry.

It spread like wildfire. Just as individuals have access to personal copies of the books they want to read, individuals everywhere had personal access to the current move of God.

Can you imagine how this enlarges the world for the Gospel? One pastor in Uganda walks two miles to the nearest village to use a cafe computer; but what a world he discovers when he gets there. Alongside the bush country where lions lie down in the heat and the sun beats down on the cracked soil, this pastor of 90 churches (churches that meet under trees) watches a healing and discovers the truth about moving in power ministry!

Elsewhere, in an extremist Muslim area of Indonesia, a family and a few friends meet secretly in a back room. Perhaps it is to watch a television or the small screen of a laptop computer. But now, they are viewing programming beyond their wildest dreams! They can watch a Harvest Rock Church conference live—and learn about taking over the mountains of their culture. As they watch the prayer time, they, too, might be hit with the power of God in salvation, healing, or personal revival.

Do you remember years back when television evangelists asked their audience members to touch their television screen to receive their healing? How about when the apostle Paul touched handkerchiefs that were placed on the sick and the anointing was released for the miracles they needed? (See Acts 19:12.)

It's happening again over the airwaves—and without limitation!

The Holy Spirit is just looking for a conduit or point of contact to transfer the anointing. Not only can teaching be shared through these media, but also miracles! Here's just one testimony from a friend of mine who was watching the "Burn Atlanta Revival" with Jim Drown:

> I was working in my kitchen with my laptop perched on the counter. I had been feeling dead on the inside and really needed a fresh dose from God. I couldn't make the morning revival meeting, but I was watching it live by streaming video. Jim Drown called out a word of knowledge that directly applied to me. I was drawn to touch the screen of my laptop even though he never asked. I just felt the Holy Spirit leading me to do it!
>
> The power of God hit me so hard, I felt like I had been wonderfully electrocuted with the awesome love and glory of God. I started screaming!
>
> I could tell that God was delivering me of something, and frankly, I was glad I wasn't in the meeting so I didn't scare everyone else! I felt a horrible oppression leave me. God's presence was stronger on me than when someone had touched me in prayer in person and I had been slain in the Spirit. I was amazed, and am still changed by it today!

We so believe that Jesus wants us to reach uncountable masses with these media that we have invested in 24/7 website, video streaming networks, and programming on God TV and other channels such as the Australian Christian Channel. God TV alone has a potential household viewing audience of millions in more than 215 nations! The Australian channel extends to 150 countries! Our show *The Holy Spirit Today*, reaches far lands and the shut-in down the street. We also broadcast our special events, outreaches, and conferences. This vastly expands our Harvest International network's capacity to reach the world for Christ and change countless lives.

While it had been prophesied many years before that we would be involved in the media, it took ten years to come to pass. Yet already the results are staggering.

Our Australian apostle says his network has increased from four to 40 churches—and he believes that is directly attributable to our television program being aired there. We have even gained a powerful new HIM member pastor in India who had been watching our show in Dubai! Moreover, this medium gives us ready access to train our 5,000 member churches and keep them current in the river of God. One of the most difficult dilemmas of revival is being able to teach new believers in distant lands. It is hard to provide written materials or on-location teachers.

Through media, the same world-class teaching we receive right here in the United States can be given to newly-saved believers huddled in a hut in India or crammed in a huge underground meeting in China. And it costs the viewer nothing! The basics of the foundations of Christianity can be firmly established in a much shorter time period than in years past and at far less cost. While a dollar can hardly buy stamps enough to reach two households, a satellite beam has expansive reach unduplicated by any other means!

There is no distance in the Spirit, and as technology increases, we are believing God for the means to hold live, two-way, interactive conferences all over the globe. A Vineyard pastor who is also a businessman invented and patented the most high-tech form of this communication and has now sold it to the largest Fortune 500 companies.

More Inventions

Recently, solar-powered DVDs have been produced. These are being used to share the ever-successful *Jesus Video* in the Amazon and other places where lack of electricity and the limitations of canoe transport make it difficult to take in equipment.

With solar technology and portable, sheet-like video screens, native tribesman can see images displayed before them for the first time! Imagine the exponential increase in the demonstration and understanding of the Gospel—especially among unreached peoples for whom translated materials are not available. With a minimum of equipment and the presence of just one person familiar with the languages involved, translation becomes an easy challenge to overcome.

Another current "pocket miracle" is being able to download a translation of the entire Bible onto an iPod. This small-sized wonder not only draws the interest of remote peoples; it also allows many to study together while listening through a tiny speaker. No electricity is needed!

You've no doubt heard of the "cell phone miracles" that have been flooding meetings since Lakeland. While the anointing is strong and believers are crowded together in prayer and the glory, attendees call friends in need and prayer is ministered over the phone.

Just a few testimonies of which I am aware include a 19-year-old boy who had been in a coma for two years. His father was called; he took the phone and placed it on the boy's heart. As prayer went forth, the boy awoke! He is still awake and slowly recovering. All the medical personnel working with him are amazed!

Another person called her husband, who was severely depressed. The instant he received prayer, he felt the oppression leave him. The testimonies are endless. Cell phones have a greater use than that of kids sharing after-school gossip!

I thought I'd end this chapter by sharing just a few more testimonies we have received from those who wrote or called us about our program *The Holy Spirit Today.*

One woman in Malawi, Africa, was saddened and fearful when she lost her job. As I was sharing on a program about a dream the Lord had given me of future ministry plans, God gave her a similar experience about a new job.

Her miracle came about just as she had "seen" it. She shared here joy saying, "Thank you, Ché Ahn, for your testimony. You don't know how it has moved my heart."

A teen from Canada wrote of his newfound conviction to make things right with people he had wounded through a series of dangerous and selfish sins. The young man decided to do what was right "even if it means prison."

A man from Sudan living in Alberta shared how "he was full of anger and bitterness" toward the Muslims around whom he had been raised and tortured as a captured child soldier. Upon meeting Christ and also hearing many of the teachings on our show, God changed his heart; he recently returned to Sudan to preach to his former enemies!

One of my staff members took a call from a former Muslim who had been watching our show and decided to accept "Jesus as his personal Lord and Savior." The staffer jotted down the details of the call on a sheet of paper and added a note to me saying, "These may just look like words on a page (to you) but if you could have heard the excitement in his voice, the hunger, and the childlike desire! A television show is a great thing, but it is not *just* a television show. It is a vehicle that is … changing lives!"

Let the media mania continue! Let God use you to create testimonies the world needs to hear!

Endnotes

1. Mary Bellis, "Johannes Gutenberg and the Printing Press," *About.com,* http://inventors.about.com/od/gstartinvetors/a/Gutenberg.htm (accessed March 19, 2009).

2. Steven Strader, *The Lakeland Outpouring: The Inside Story* (Windermere, FL: Legacy Media Group Publishing, 2008), 34.

CHAPTER 12

From Renewal to Revival

I t has been a privilege to share so many wonderful experiences of my life with you. I am also grateful for the opportunity to speak of those who have influenced my life and who those who have "run with the ball" God has placed in our hands.

We have witnessed the wonders that happen when we yield to Jesus and simply follow Him as He follows the Father. We have seen how the Lord is refreshing us personally in our hope, strength, and vision (renewal) and how He has moved us into corporate revival. As we have seen, this process most recently began in the early 1990s in Toronto.

Recently, in talking with revivalists and world-changers Pastor Bill Johnson and Pastor John Arnott of Toronto, we revisited some fascinating facts about the history of renewal and revival.

Many people have heard of the historic Azusa Street Revival in Los Angeles in 1906. Yet few realize that more people have been filled with the Holy Spirit in the Toronto move of God than were Spirit-filled during the Azusa Street Revival.

More souls have been saved, too. Azusa averaged 300 people a day and lasted a few years. In its time, nothing like it had ever been seen. Many came from overseas and took back what they had received from the meetings, spreading the experience of speaking in tongues and the infilling of the Holy Spirit to the nations.

Toronto has now lasted 12 years with more than 4 million visitors. Many people have continually used the word "renewal" to describe this move of God, but upon review of the facts and the fruit, we have changed our estimation and see Toronto as a revival. Revival is more long lasting, involves more people, and brings more change.

We are still waiting for great revival in many places so that hearts and lives may be changed. With revival comes the *"restoration of all things"* (Acts 3:21). We are beginning to see this manifestation along with transformation. We are seeing the *"summing up of all things in Christ"* (Eph. 1:10 NASB).

However, my heart will not be fully released until I make an appeal to you to ensure that Christianity does not return to a powerless state and to ensure that neither you nor your children find yourselves unchanged by the God of all.

My appeal is twofold. The first point is a caution: revival and personal refreshment must not be seen as desired ends. If revival and personal refreshment are seen as spiritual endpoints, their fires can burn out without leaving any permanent change. While we are to enjoy these experiences to the fullest and bring everyone we know into contact with such outpourings, there is more.

The second aspect of this appeal is that we must go on to the *reformation* of society. I believe that is ultimately what is on God's heart.

He gave His Son, not only for a few to be blessed, but so that nations are discipled (see Matt. 28:18-20). I use the word *reformation* rather than transformation. Cindy Jacobs, in her best-selling book *The Reformation Manifesto,* explains why we need reformation and not just transformation:

The Bible is full of answers for transforming society! However, if we transform without putting reformational laws, structures, and a biblical worldview in our everyday lives, society will revert to its former state.[1]

It is not enough to have sustained revival. We do need to contend for that, but I have seen revival in Africa and India where countless millions of souls have reportedly been saved. Yet for the most part, society has not changed. We need to bring reformation to nations that are experiencing revival. To use our own nation as an example: if reformation merely meant seeing people born-again, having many churches, or faithfully attending church, then Dallas, Texas, would be one of the most godly, successful cities in the world! Sadly, it is not. Dallas has so many Christians producing little social impact. It takes more to change humanity and culture than salvation alone.

Cindy goes on to define reformation:

I would define reformation as an amendment to repair what is corrupt, to build the institutions of our governments and society according to their God-ordained order and organization. It means to institutionalize God's will in how we do our daily business, deal with the poor, administer justice, make our laws, teach our children, and generally live our lives.[2]

That is why, in this chapter, I desire to entrust you with insight and challenge you to be a part of social reformation. Sadly, there are few modern-day examples of cities that have experienced sustained social transformation (reformation). That means there are few experts to lead the way, and I am not claiming to be one of them. But I offer to you what I have seen make an impact that most often leads to reformation.

There have been some cities, such as Almolonga in the Central American nation of Guatemala, where sustained revival and Christian involvement to bring governmental change has also served to shut down bars and empty out jails. Today, institutions that used to house criminals are being used as wedding chapels. Marriages are being restored due to deliverance from alcoholism. There have been dramatic changes in economics and education. More than 80 percent of Almolonga is now Christian, and God's favor is seen through unusual growth and profits in agriculture. Farmers are delivering their abundant harvests in Mercedes trucks![3]

How awesome! We just need more! I talk about revival coming before reformation because, just as is in Almolonga, there has not been (to my knowledge) an example of true social reformation without the Spirit of revival coming on people first.

The best illustration is the Great Awakening. This outpouring led to the abolishment of slavery in England. When people's hearts were changed, the nation changed, too—and in lasting ways.

This kind of change doesn't happen without preparation. We have to prepare the hearth of our hearts for revival. Just as we prepare our homes for a very important guest, we need to prepare ourselves, our churches, and our cities for His arrival. After all, that is what revival is— His arrival.

How do we prepare for revival?

There is no way, in this limited space, to do justice to the huge subjects of revival and reformation. Not surprisingly, there are untold volumes written, some at great length, on the subject. I can, however, share some principles I've learned and hopefully help you gain a vision for reformation.

I'll just share what I call "The Cycle of Revival and Reformation." I call the process a cycle because we are never intended to arrive at the end of any particular stage. Rather, we are to evolve and delve deeper and deeper into the process.

Seek Personal Renewal and Extended Revival

Many people have experienced renewal or refreshing as well as sustained revival in places such as Toronto, Canada (Toronto Airport Christian Fellowship); Redding, California (Bethel Church); Denton,

Texas (Glory of Zion Church); Pasadena, California (Harvest Rock Church); and other places around North America and the world.

Yet, history tells us that, for one reason or another, people tend to lose interest in pursuing revival at some point. A "been there, done that" mentality can set in and hinder us from moving into greater revival and change. That attitude affects more than just our personal lives; it affects outcomes in our cities, nations, and world.

This is also one of the chief dangers for those who have had these spiritual experiences. Too often, people want to be involved for the "pleasurable" aspects and not for the transformation. We are to go all the way into the flow of Jesus. We are to *stay there* and bring others into the waters with us. This is how we will see this earth and its structures become Christ's.

Ezekiel 47 describes the water level rising in the Temple and flowing out into the Dead Sea in an ever-increasing measure. This water level is analogous to the flow of God. Note that Ezekiel did not go into the river only to become disinterested and walk away.

Rather, he stayed in the river until the water was so deep that it could not be crossed (see Ezek. 47:1-5). We all must hunger for more! One thing I especially like to note in this passage was that the water was "over their heads." (The phrase "a river that no one can cross" implies that the water was over their heads.) In other words, it was no longer about men's notions, *their* thinking and plans (i.e., what was in their heads). Rather they were "flooded" by the waves of God alone. They were no longer able to move about in their own plans and directions, but were swept along with God's current and direction.

This is a distinction worth noting because many people venture into His refreshing and change—the new things of God—but go only ankle- or waist-deep. Some may even go in up to their shoulders, yet they begin to reason their way out of the river and decide they don't need any more of God.

I believe we're not in deep enough water until we are truly in over our heads and aware that we are no longer in control—only God is. Once you've experienced this level of surrender to God and have seen the success and fruit it brings, you can't help but want more. As revivalist John Arnott says in *The Father's Blessing:*

> We are saying, "Oh, Holy Spirit, we are not satisfied with what we have. It is wonderful. You have increased the anointing. You have increased the power, but oh God, let there be more. Let people be so filled with You that we will see the lame walk, the blind see, the deaf hear, the dead raised and the poor of the world have the gospel preached to them." That is where the Father wants to take us.[4]

This righteous dissatisfaction does not mean that we are ungrateful receivers. Rather we are being hungry recipients. After all, Jesus said "[we] *have not, because* [we] *ask not*" (James 4:2 KJV).

Are we that *filled?* Are we that *hungry?* I believe God wants us to experience the refreshing waters of renewal and then stay in the waters until they rise to the historic levels of revival that bring a deeper and greater intimacy with the Father.

How can we walk away from something as wonderful as that? If revival gives forth such a fresh and mighty infilling of the Holy Spirit—and it does!—why would anyone want to cut it off?

Unfortunately, many do cut it off. I have learned, however, that I must have that deep drink every day; I need it to survive and to be continually filled with the Holy Spirit (see Eph. 5:18). I believe the same is true for all of us, without exception! That is why I will endeavor to make personal ministry time at every service in order to pray for people to be filled afresh with the Holy Spirit. I do this at Harvest Rock Church and encourage all of our HIM churches to do the same. Whenever I am invited to minister elsewhere, I strive to make that time of personal ministry available.

You can never have too much of God. Ephesians 5:18 exhorts us to *"be filled with the Spirit."* The form of the verb *to be filled* means a continuous action of "being filled to overflowing" (baptized) with the Spirit. The Greek word *baptizo,* literally means to "make overwhelmed"; while another synonym, *bapto,* means "to cover wholly with a fluid; to stain or to dye."[5]

To me, that sounds like an ongoing flood of God Himself! As we give the anointing away, we need more. We also leak as we walk through this unredeemed world. That is why we need more than an occasional "dose" of God's presence; we need His incredible love through the filling of His Spirit every day.

On the broader scale, we need to pursue revival corporately. This means the pursuit, not just of individuals, but of the Church as a whole. This is how the Church will profoundly influence the world and usher in mass salvations.

As we are faithful in pursuit of both renewal and revival, I believe we can expect even more to result from our seeking (see Luke 16:10). Seek it out; and keep seeking. Receive as much prayer as you can, and give as much away as you can. When we are full of the Holy Spirit and in love with Jesus, then we are empowered and desirous to move into the next phase of the cycle.

If you have not experienced renewal, then go where you can receive personal prayer and a new infilling of the Holy Spirit by faith. Go to one of the "watering holes" mentioned in the first paragraph of this section.

If you have *never* experienced the awesome manifestations of being filled with the Holy Spirit, pursue them. Although I believe we all receive a measure of the Holy Spirit when we are saved, the Word says there is a *baptism* in the Holy Spirit (see Acts 1:5; 11:16). I believe this deeper and more complete immersing is a separate and conscious act for every believer. While there may be a corporate filling or refreshing at a large meeting, there is a personal infilling for every believer; it is an infilling that lasts for a lifetime.

When we are thus filled, it is easy for all of the signs that follow believers (see Mark 16:17) to spill forth from us day in and day out. The Great Commission, as Jesus described it, should be commonplace for all believers:

> In My name they will cast out demons; they will speak with new tongues; they will take up serpents; and if they drink anything deadly, it will by no means hurt them; they will lay hands on the sick, and they will recover (Mark 16:17-18).

According to the Lord, this is simply evidence of a Christian life. Our experience in the supernatural should not be occasional or the "exception"; it should be the norm. As someone has said, we often think we are human beings living a temporary spiritual existence. The truth is that we are spiritual beings living a temporary human existence! As you live out this one change in mindset, it will change your world and the world around you forever.

We are to be the trendsetters, the mind-molders, and *the* example for others. That is why God gave us dominion in this world—and that is why He is eager to give greater revelation to those who hunger to know how that supernatural mindset looks in our daily lives.

For far too long, the Church has allowed the world to dictate the standards when, in fact, the world has no truth to share. True change will begin when the Church—as individuals and as a Body—takes its ordained place in the world.

Prepare for a Great Harvest

We need to "prepare the nets" on the Kingdom level, the apostolic level, and the local level. We talked about apostolic alignment (every church having an apostolic link for foundational building), but let's examine getting the nets ready in a local church.

If God gave us a great harvest overnight, could we handle it? What would we do with all those who came in? Are our "nets" prepared, or will they break under the strain? Could we handle the fish as well as "clean" and care for them?

I was saved during the Jesus Movement in the early 1970s, and I observed thousands more receive Christ in those days. Yet many of them fell away because churches were not ready to handle the harvest. We need churches that can incorporate, care for, and disciple new believers. Then, as trained believers, they need to be released as laborers into the harvest. It takes a process to do that. The Holy Spirit will lead you, but we must participate in the preparation. I believe the time is now to train for the harvest!

I also believe every saint must be equipped for the work of the ministry (see Eph. 4:11). At Harvest Rock Church, we encourage new people to attend our new members' class. By attending and completing the new members' class, they receive a strong foundation in becoming committed, not only to Jesus, but also to the church. In our new members' seminars, we emphasize the importance of getting involved in a cell group or a small home group. We are also able to bring everyone onto the "same page" with the vision of the church and with what each member brings to the table.

I believe the emphasis on small groups or cell groups is what the Holy Spirit is saying to the worldwide Church today. The cell structure is the best way to retain the harvest. Included in the cell structure is personal, ongoing discipleship of cell leaders and other leaders in the church.

Our cell leaders usually meet in group settings once a month, but there is ongoing, clear accountability and alignment. These kinds of meetings and this type of structure addresses the need for deep, meaningful, personal relationships in the Church. This is an element that has been missing from many church settings.

At Harvest Rock Church, Sunday morning is an equipping time and not just a time to bless the church. Again, we are to equip the saints for ministry. Because we live in Los Angeles, where it is difficult for families to fight traffic, fix dinner, and attend a class or some other type of session designed to equip the saints, we have these kinds of meetings on the weekends. We have our Harvest School of Ministry before our Sunday morning service.

We also have our Wagner Leadership Institute for those who want to get their diploma as either a Master or Doctor of Practical Ministry; most of these classes take place on weekends.

I also believe in a mentoring model. Those who are prophets should train and mentor prophets; apostles and those with other gifting should do likewise. I am not so much advocating our model; of course, if it is helpful to you, that is wonderful! Rather, I am suggesting application of a diligent and progressive system designed to effectively process the harvest.

Whatever the system, it must encompass every level of the local church, and it must be felt throughout. The most important element of any system is that we bring people into a loving community of believers.

People are looking for a sense of belonging. Consider the gang problems among the youth. These kids believe they don't belong in their homes or in society. Most have no personal family life. They seek to fill the need for family and community by joining gangs!

Therefore, we need to become that family for all those who come to Christ. The church is an army, but it is a family first. We must demonstrate the love and care and sense of family to effectively receive the harvest.

Plant New Churches

On another level, we need to plant as many new churches as possible. C. Peter Wagner has said that church planting is the most effective way of evangelizing the lost.[6] That is why we have formed the apostolic network called Harvest International Ministry. We want to fulfill the Great Commission by planting as many churches as possible before the Lord comes.

Kingdom Unity

Finally, let me encourage apostolic networks, ministries and denominations to pull together and unite their efforts to reach and receive the harvest.

Several of us have already formed The Revival Alliance. Bill Johnson, John Arnott, Heidi Baker, Randy Clark, Georgian Banov, and I spend time talking together regularly to sharpen our faith and gain wisdom from each other to help usher in revival to the nations through our respective networks. I would encourage others to do the same.

The Bible says we have increased levels of exponential strength every time we work together! (See Deuteronomy 32:30.)

Endnotes

1. Cindy Jacobs, *The Reformation Manifesto* (Bloomington, MN: Bethany House Publishers, 2008), 14.

2. *Ibid.,* 18.

3. For more on this, watch *Transformations I: A Documentary* by George Otis Jr. of the Sentinel Group. It is available at http://www.sentinelgroup.org/videos.asp.

4. John Arnott, *The Father's Blessing* (Lake Mary, FL: Creation House, 1995).

5. Colin Brown, ed., *New International Dictionary of New Testament Theology,* vol. 1 (Grand Rapids, MI: Zondervan, 1986), 144.

6. C. Peter Wagner, *Dominion* (Grand Rapids, MI: Chosen Books, 2008), 56.

CHAPTER 13

Reformation

What It Is and Why It Begins With You

As I mentioned in the previous chapter, there is a significant difference between revival and reformation. I quoted Cindy Jacobs who sees "reformation as an amendment to repair what is corrupt, to build the institutions of our governments and society according to their God-ordained order and organization. It means to institutionalize God's will in how we do our daily business, deal with the poor, administer justice, make our laws, teach our children, and generally live our lives."[1]

Reformation is a hard-fought encompassing sweep to bring God's order where humanistic man has staked his claim and definition. Yet it begins one person at a time.

I would like to leave you not only with the knowledge that *you are significant,* but also with the assurance that you have *a powerful Christianity*— a living faith that will help you to make the changes needed to ensure that God's holy name is made known and honored in our generation.

So, let's begin with you.

Stage 1: Pursue Personal Reformation Through Holiness And Wholeness

The Bible says that *"... without holiness, no one will see the Lord"* (Heb. 12:14 NIV).We will not experience revival and social reformation without the condition of personal and corporate holiness.

Throughout revival history, we observe that holiness was a major condition for revival. Charles Finney (an American evangelist and revivalist during the Second Great Awakening (1792-1875), said that revival is "nothing else than a new beginning of obedience to God."[2] Biblically, we notice how repentance precedes revival in passages such as Second Chronicles 7:14; Joel 2:12-32; Acts 2:38; and Acts 3:19.

I emphasize holiness as being foundational to reformation because I have seen too many people in important (or foundational) positions in our society fall because of character or wholeness issues. Sadly, this is not just a Church issue; it also greatly affects the arenas of government, business, and finance, to name a few.

We will not see reformation without holiness.

Allow me to explain what I mean by being "holy." Positionally speaking, all believers are holy *now*. The Bible says we are *"a holy nation"* (1 Pet. 2:9). We are made holy by the blood of the Lamb and by His sacrifice to grant us salvation. However, God wants us to be holy *in practice*. To be holy, then, means to be set apart and to cease practicing *"the sin that so easily entangles"* us (Heb. 12:1).

We cannot do this in our own strength. Be honest with God and admit to Him that you cannot overcome any sin apart from His grace and strength. By grace you were saved, and by grace you will continue being saved from each and every hindrance to serving the Lord in purity and holiness (see Eph. 2:8).

What we can do is ask God to help us be *aware* of our sins. Then we must repent of every sin He shows us. Repentance then causes us to hate and forsake our sins. It is laying our sins on the altar and letting the fire of God consume them. It is dying to those sins on the Cross daily and not returning to them. One of the best ways is to love God more than you "love" the sinful activity; then you will find sin beginning to lose its appeal.

When I repent, I may say something like, "Father, I have this anger toward my brother. I cannot change myself, but I come to You to receive grace and mercy by faith. I repent of the sin of anger, and I ask for Your forgiveness. I come to Your Cross, and I ask You to help me crucify this anger on the Cross. By faith, I receive Your forgiveness and deliverance in Jesus' name, and I forgive my brother as well."

I think this is what it means to take up the Cross daily and what it means to confess your sins. It is then that He will forgive you and deliver you from your sin (see 1 John 1:9). By doing this with every sin, every time we sin, we learn to pray without ceasing, and we practice the presence of the Holy Spirit. I believe this continuous process is what it means to be thoroughly right with God and to practice holiness.

Sometimes, however, we are not aware of our sins. It is then that we need others to help us, especially those who have the gift of counseling. This is especially important when you find yourself in a continual struggle with the same issues—in relationships, your personal life, or in your character. We each have blind spots. Often these blind spots form around flaws in our character; others may try to point these flaws out to us, yet we tend to disbelieve what they claim to be true.

The Bible says that healing comes through confessing our faults to one another, through speaking the truth in love, and through humbly receiving input because we consider others more important than ourselves (see James 5:16; Eph. 4:15; Phil. 2:3).

If you find yourself bound by besetting sins, you may truly be in need of revelation; this will help you to discover the root of the sin and be healed of it. There is no higher form of freedom than that which is gained by the Master's skillful touch—often in areas where we did not even know we had a need or had missed the mark.

I highly recommend Elijah House Ministries founded by John and Paula Sandford and the Kylstras' Healing House Network. Their teaching and counsel eternally changed my own life as well as that of my family and our church.

You can also contact our church at harvestrockchurch.org. We have numerous ministries that could be a resource for you. We are also certified to do Sozo Ministry, which was birthed from Bethel Church (Bill Johnson) out of Redding, California.

Stage 2: Enter Into Extraordinary Prayer and Fasting Over Cities

I once heard someone say that historical revival has never taken place without united prayer being first on the agenda. We all know that prayer is an indispensable condition for revival, but do we realize that it is crucial for reformation?

As you saw in the chapter about TheCall and the results of TheCall, prayer does bring reforming change—to law, to leadership, to all of society's institutions.

How shall we pray? Paul gives us the answer:

> I urge, then, **first of all,** that requests, prayers, intercession and thanksgiving be made **for everyone—for kings and all those in authority,** that we may live peaceful and quiet lives in all godliness and holiness (1 Timothy 2:1-2 NIV, emphasis added).

Every day, you have the privilege of praying for revival and for the lost (see 1 Tim. 2:1-4). Paul is clear that we are also to pray for *"kings and all those in authority."* This is reformational prayer. Keep in mind that Nero, perhaps the most wicked emperor in Roman history, was emperor at the time Paul wrote this epistle.

How many of us pray for our president every day? How many of us pray for corporate leaders or for our bosses? Yes, pray for your pastor! These people are in positions of servant leadership; God can change history by changing their hearts, whether they be leaders in national government, business, entertainment, or any other field.

God is also raising up intercessors for government leaders and CEOs. My friend, Tommie Femrite, has established a ministry that will mobilize intercessors for CEOs around the world. There are prayer groups praying for Hollywood to be transformed into "Holywood." We must have prayer groups and intercessors for every type of leader that God is raising up to climb the seven mountains of culture and bring His standards and His change.

There can be no transformation without a prayer strategy. This must include prayer for everything from identificational repentance (the praying for forgiveness of past or present besetting sins of a nation)—as seen in Daniel 9, Nehemiah 9, and Ezra 9—to strategic warfare for the general direction of nations. C. Peter Wagner has written a great deal on this subject. I highly recommend his latest book *Praying with Power;* it covers much of what I am talking about in this section.

As my good friend Lou Engle has said, "There cannot be sustained transformation of society until we raise up a House of Prayer that will contend with all the other houses." Prayer is essential to transformation.

Finally, we must target cities. We are called to disciple nations, but I believe that we need to start with a realistic goal of transforming cities. In his book *That None Should Perish,* Ed Silvoso points out the importance of reaching cities:

> Cities are central to God's redemptive strategy. The Great Commission begins with a city—Jerusalem—and culminates when another city—the New Jerusalem—becomes God's eternal dwelling with His people. In order to fulfill the Great Commission, we must reach every city on earth with the gospel.[3]

Unified extraordinary prayer and a strategy for reaching cities are major steps to reformation.

All of it begins with you!

Stage 3: Establish Networks That *Work*

In his *Revival Lectures,* Charles Finney said that two basic conditions are necessary for revival: prayer and unity.[4] Of course, the unity of which he spoke is the unity of the Church.

D.L. Moody, the famed 19th-century urban revivalist, said in his book *Secret Power:* "I never yet have known the Spirit of God to work where the Lord's people were divided."[5]

I believe unity occurs on several levels. First, we should be reconciled to others—period. An abundance of Bible verses speak of forgiveness and reconciliation; we need not belabor the point. Instead, we must just do it! We need to be reconciled—brothers to brothers, fathers to sons, and husbands to wives—to be at peace with all men *"... as far as it depends on you... "* (Rom. 12:18 NIV).

Second, unity and love must be apparent within a local church. God is purging the Church of slander, gossip, and criticism. He is serious about this kind of sin. If we are not part of the problem or part of the solution in a given situation, then it is not our place to get involved. We must be careful, not only about what we speak, but also about what we hear. I strongly encourage people not to speak evil of their pastors or the church leadership. Don't divide the Body and bring a reproach on him *"for whom Christ died"* (Rom. 14:15; 1 Cor. 8:11). Do not bring an accusation against an elder unless you have *"two or three witnesses"* (1 Tim. 5:19).

This is a serious hour in which God is dealing with the Church as a whole. As in the story of Achan's transgression (see Josh. 7), sin affects the whole camp and must be addressed. When one suffers, all will suffer (see 1 Cor. 12:26), so we must approach what we say and believe about others with great soberness, humility, and forgiveness. One way to encourage righteous communication and stamp out that which divides and slanders is to quit listening to those who speak such things. Kindly remind them what the Word says about it—gossip and slander are no less sinful than moral failure or other more visible sins. If there is no one to listen to such gossip, perhaps no one would speak it. You can be a reformer right in your own church!

Third, unity must exist among believers within the citywide Church. There is only one Church, regardless of denominational lines. We need to repent of any arrogance in believing that "our church" and our people are better than other churches or other people. We need to repent of sectarianism and exclusivity. The Word clearly says we will *"all come to the unity of the faith"* (Eph. 4:13); it does *not* say we will all come to a unity of doctrine.

The basics of the faith are Jesus' death and resurrection, salvation by grace and confession of belief, and the gift of eternal life through the sacrifice of our Lord. As we agree on these basics, we should not hinder each other over other matters. Instead, we need to focus on all that we can accomplish together. To bring reformation, we need all hands on deck in this last hour. We need unifiers. If we can't first see ourselves as *the* Church united in Him, we will never leave the starting gate in this effort to reform a divided and confused society.

Fourth, there must be apostolic alignment. Apostles need to come together in unity. Apostles are the highest office in the Church. We are accustomed to the title of *pastor;* too often we see them as the "end all" in Church leadership simply because we are familiar with them. Yet Scripture begs to differ. Apostles and prophets together are the foundational cornerstone with Christ, with apostles holding the chief role (see 1 Cor. 12:28). Together, the apostles and prophets present the divine overall strategy and ongoing direction for the whole Body of Christ.

When we find apostles from each sector aligned together, we will see greater anointing and greater results in transforming society; and we will see genuine revival in the Church. It is equally important for pastors to be aligned with their overseeing apostles. A lone pastor has far less influence than one who is teamed with apostolic oversight and leadership; this apostle-pastor relationship positions pastors for their greatest convergence. (Convergence is when your calling, your character, and your gifts converge together and you fulfill your destiny in God). It is time for those who lack this kind of covering to find it. This simply means seeking God for the apostolic network or "tribe" that has your DNA (the best "match" for your growth and benefit)—and then joining with those whom God has chosen for you to share covenant relationship with.

Fifth, we need to network with others to bring about reformation. The famous abolitionist William Wilberforce had a network designed to overcome slavery in England; it was called the Clapham Group. Amazingly, most members of the Clapham Group were also members of a church pastored by John Venn. Cindy Jacobs quotes Clifford Hill, an authority on the Clapham Group:

> Never have the members of one congregation so greatly influenced the history of the world. The effect of their prayers and actions not only profoundly altered the religious and social life of this country, it was also felt in Africa, in the West Indies, in India and in Austlalasia.[6]

All told, 112 members of Parliament were members of the Clapham Group. The group also included marketplace professionals such as bankers and lawyers. Both church leaders and marketplace leaders came together to pray and to take action to better society in England. They formed a network that really worked! World history was forever changed.

You have the same capacity for overcoming society's ills through networking.

Stage 4: See Yourself As a Workplace Minister

Regardless of whether we are in revival mode or not, we must realize that all believers are ministers. The Bible says that we are *"a royal priesthood"* (1 Pet. 2:9). We must understand that only 1 percent of the Church is in vocational, full-time ministry. That means 99 percent of the Church is in the workplace. It stands to reason, therefore, that most of our ministry is accomplished in the workplace. *Work* is not a four-letter curse word. Work is part of God's blessing; after all, Adam was asked to work in the Garden *before* he fell to sin.

We must make disciples in the workplace. We must evangelize in the workplace. Mark 16:15 is a mandate from our Lord, and it offers no options: we are to evangelize wherever we find people. We can become passive, believing the harvest will magically come to us—but we would be wrong to approach it that way.

Any farmer will tell you that when it is harvest time, more work is done than any other time of the year. We are to approach the harvest actively. Jesus said, *"Occupy till I come"* (Luke 19:13 KJV). He also told the disciples that we must continue to do His works while it is still day because once night comes *"no one can work"* (John 9:4).

The truth is that revival comes as we obediently do the works of God. As I said earlier, Charles Finney said revival is "nothing more than a new beginning of obedience to God."[7] We make great headway toward revival as we obey the Great Commission.

As I have shared in various chapters of this book, we are called to take our place as leaders on the mountains of society where God has placed us or is calling us to be. Whether it is education or the arts, economy or religion, government, the media, or family, it is time for us to take dominion—God's fullest call to His people on this earth. Only then is He truly represented and honored as Lord of all. Only then are His ways are established. That is how we move beyond a mere visitation of the Lord to both demonstrate and become His *habitation*.

Stage 5: Realize It Takes Money to Bring Reformation

I have learned that it takes money (lots of it!) to bring about the reformation of society. Many people don't like to hear this. However, just as God chose to use money to reveal man's heart and his priorities (according to Matthew 6:24 and Luke 16:13, you cannot serve two masters), He chose money as a means of power to change society for good or for evil.

It is God's choice to use money to help fulfill the Great Commission. In his book *Dominion,* C. Peter Wagner says, "If you check back through history, you will find that three things, more than any others, have produced social transformation: violence, knowledge and wealth—and the greatest of these is wealth!"[8]

To illustrate how these principles bring about a measure of reformation, let's look again at Proposition 8 recently passed in California. This proposition defined marriage exclusively as a union between one man and one woman. Seeing this proposition passed took tremendous effort. We had strong leadership, like my good friend Pastor Jim Garlow, who mobilized 3,000 pastors in California to help get out the evangelical Christian vote.

But I learned that the networking had to reach beyond evangelical Christians. There was tremendous networking among like-minded Roman Catholics, Mormons, and people of every race and color. There was a massive prayer and fasting initiative, including TheCall San Diego, with Lou Engle leading the charge.

Yet it took millions and millions of dollars to bring about victory. Expensive television advertising was a necessity to counter the heavily budgeted opposition and win the hearts of voters. I heard that this was the most expensive proposition campaign in the history of California. More than $80 million dollars was raised; $43 million by those opposed and $39.9 million by those in favor of Proposition 8. I am convinced that if we as proponents of the proposition had not raised the needed funds, we would have lost the campaign for this measure. Money is the currency of society. It takes money to transform society; and we must be willing to support godly causes if we truly seek to honor God. As His servant David said, *"I will not give to God that which costs me nothing"* (see 2 Sam. 24:24).

He created us as givers not only to purify our hearts and make us glad in our giving, but also to help us decide our future by choosing what we are willing to support.

There is one more major requirement for achieving lasting change.

Stage 6: Establish Transformation-Sustaining Laws, Worldviews, and Structures

There is a distinct difference between transformation and reformation. A transformation is the process that changes something from one form into another form. Reformation is the infrastructure that supports transformation; reformation establishes, sustains, and promotes its growth.

God never intended for Christians to "occupy" temporarily. Just as He intends to inhabit us and not just visit us, He intends for us to bring reformation and not just temporary change. That is truly our call to take dominion and *"see the kingdoms of this world... become the kingdoms of... His Christ"* (Rev. 11:15).

Here's just one example of what I mean: as soon as Proposition 8 was passed in California, the opposition submitted three lawsuits against the state to reverse the vote. Major government leaders (including Governor Schwarzenegger) expressed their disappointment over the proposition's passage and declared their commitment to overturn the people's vote.

This is an example of history repeating itself; this wasn't the first time Californians had voted to define marriage as the union between one man and one woman. The first time was in 2000, when Proposition 22 was on the ballot and the people of California voted in favor of it—overwhelmingly.

Sadly, there was no infrastructure in place to sustain the people's vote. The gay community sued the State of California, and the case finally went to the State Supreme Court. In April 2008, activist judges voted to overturn the wishes of more than 60 percent of voters and legalize same-sex marriages. This is why infrastructure is so vital.

However, in California you can reverse a Supreme Court decision if you have a sufficient number of people sign a petition to place the measure on the ballot for the next election. That is exactly what happened with Proposition 8. This illustrates how important it is to enact lasting laws to prevent the legalization of same-sex marriage from becoming a repeat issue or enduring standard of life.

First, there must be revival to change people's hearts to have a biblical world view; then societal structures must be built and legislated to firmly establish a once-and-for-all biblical understanding of marriage. This is why reformation of society is so vital.

Another example is the effort to eliminate systemic poverty. I agree with city strategist and apostolic minister Ed Silvoso that the elimination of systemic poverty is one indicator of true social transformation.

When the U.S. government began the War on Poverty in 1965, 12 percent of American people were considered to be poor. We have spent more than $3 billion to wipe out poverty. Yet, after all the billions that have been spent, we still have a poverty rate of 12 percent!

C. Peter Wagner quotes Senator Sam Brownback of Kansas regarding what is needed to end poverty:

> The key to ending poverty is getting at least a minimal education, getting married, not having children until you are married, and keeping your child. The number of people in poverty that have done these four basic things is very, very small.[9]

What Sam Brownback is talking about is dealing with the root of poverty and the need to educate people with a basic Judeo-Christian worldview. Combine this with the right structures in society to eradicate systemic poverty and you will see lasting change!

This is why Cindy Jacobs calls for reformation of society and for every believer to be a reformer.

The Next "Chapter"

I know that I have just touched the surface of the subject on revival, transformation, and reformation, but I felt no peace in ending this book without looking at the next "chapter" for all of us.

I am excited to see that so many of us are hearing what the Holy Spirit is saying to the churches. I believe that we will hear of more and more cities and nations experiencing sustained transformation and reformation of society as indeed the *"the kingdoms of this world... become the kingdoms of... His Christ"* (Rev. 11:15)—and He is glorified!

We each have a choice. I would like to believe that every one of you reading this book desires to be like the wise investor who received more talents as the reward for his shrewd investment (see Matt. 25). It is my hope that no one who reads these pages would be content to live a life of inaction and become a "cursed fig tree" (see Mark 11:13-14) or a *"wicked, lazy servant"* (Matt. 25:26 NIV). I don't think you would have even picked up this book if that outcome were possible! *I'm believing you are what God believes you are—a significant and powerful Christian who desires to devote your life to godly change and eternal glory.*

As we help to usher in His second coming, we find ourselves one step closer each day to seeing His glorious face and hearing His words: *"Well done, good and faithful servant!"* (Matt. 25:21 NIV). Every tear will be wiped off the faces of all who have suffered on this earth, and the fullness of joy will be our portion forever as we rule and reign with Him.

May revival and reformation come and continue to transform your life, your family, and society—for indeed, the best is yet to come!

Endnotes

1. Cindy Jacobs, *The Reformation Manifesto* (Bloomington, MN: Bethany House Publishers), 18.

2. Charles Finney, *Revival Lectures* (Grand Rapids, MI; Fleming H. Revell Company, n.d.), 7.

3. Ed Silvoso, *That None Should Perish* (Ventura, CA: Regal Books, 1994), 21.

4. Finney, 349.

5. Dwight L. Moody, *Secret Power* (Ventura, CA: Regal Books, 1987), 124.

6. Jacobs, 143.

7. Finney, 7.

8. C. Peter Wagner, *Dominion* (Grand Rapids, MI: Chosen Books, 2008), 181.

9. Wagner, 177.

Epilogue

Perhaps the greatest pleasure in writing this book is the privilege of sharing with each of you the greatest truth of release and rest I know: *let go and let God.*

Get in the river of God, and let it flow over your head so all you can do is move in His current. Then stay there!

For so many years, I lived the world's mentality that posits, "If I don't do it, it won't get done." Actually, if it is just me doing it, I am in great danger.

It thrills me to live each day following the Lord's lead. I am forever grateful that He shows us this very important truth: His life operating through us enables us to do anything He asks us to do. It is just as He said: *"Without Me, you can do nothing"* (John 15:5).

Thus, I've come to learn that the greatest leaders are the greatest followers. I add this as a postscript for your meditation. God is no respecter of men or women. There are many things you may have read in this book that sparked your interest, kindled your dreams, or drew desire from deep within you. That is because you were made for significance of the highest order: you were made in His image. You come into the fullness of His image by following Him.

It is my hope and prayer that the revelation and examples found in these pages will free you to live a powerful life in your Christianity. You have been given all you need for life and godliness (see 2 Peter 1:3). The wisdom lies in *how you use it.*

May you and our most generous God be blessed. May He be honored as we find our significance, become filled with His power, and fulfill our design and destinies.

To do so would be pleasing to Him and ever so awesome for us. To God be all the glory!

APPENDIX

The Reformer's Pledge
Ché Ahn

As a lover and disciple of Jesus Christ, I am called to be a re-former, world-changer, and history-maker (see Acts 13:36). As a reformer, I pledge to advance His Kingdom, fulfill the Great Commission, and live for the glory of God. By His grace, power, and authority, I also pledge the following:

1. I will live a life of love, constantly receiving the love of my heavenly Father; and in return, I will love God and love my neighbor as myself (see Matt. 22:37-39).

2. I will lead a holy life, constantly growing in personal wholeness and godly character so that I will please God and not disqualify myself from fulfilling my destiny as a reformer (see 1 Pet. 1:15-16).

3. I will give myself to prayer since I am part of the house of prayer for all nations. I will intercede for those who are in authority over the seven mountains of culture. Through prayer, I will spiritually contend with all false religions and false ideologies. I will also pray for the peace of Jerusalem

and pray that all of Israel will be saved (see Mark 11:17; Ps. 122:6; Acts 1:8).

4. I will contend for revival in the Church and spiritual awakening in my nation; and I will continually be filled with the power of the Holy Spirit (see Joel 2:28).

5. I will contend for the rights of the unborn until abortion is illegal and rare. I will not vote for anyone who is pro-choice (see Exod. 20:13).

6. I will focus on strengthening and prioritizing my own family and will not allow the sacred covenant of marriage between a man and a woman to be constitutionally redefined (see Gen. 2:24).

7. I will fight racism and social injustice, care for God's planet, and do all that I can to eradicate systemic poverty through my sphere of influence (see Matt. 6:9-10).

8. I will discover which of the seven mountains of culture (education, government, media, the economy, religion, arts and entertainment, and family) God has designed me to climb, and I will do my part to bring sustained social transformation to those areas to which I am called (see Matt. 28:18-20).

9. I will be generous with the time, finances, gifts, and talents God has entrusted to me in order to bring about the reformation of society (see Luke 19:11-26).

10. I will love God's Church, walk in unity with God's people, and be in proper alignment and covering with: those who are in spiritual authority in my life, those who work beside me in serving the Lord, and those who are entrusted to my oversight. I will pursue unity, alignment, and righteousness within these relationships, knowing that this cohesion in the Body of Christ is necessary to reform society (see Ps. 133).

Author's Ministry Contact

For more information about the author's ministry, please visit the following websites:

www.cheahn.org

www.Harvestrockchurch.org

www.harvestim.org